WALKS IN REIVER COUNTRY

Northumberland
NATIONAL PARK

Produced and published by Northumberland
County Council National Park Division,
Eastburn, South Park, Hexham, Northumberland
NE46 1BS.

The National Park gratefully acknowledges the
Forestry Commission, the Ministry of Defence,
the National Trust and all landowners and
farmers who agreed to walks on their land.
The route for Walk 13 was researched by Alan
Hall, National Park Wardens selected the other
routes and field staff carried out stiling and
waymarking.

Text by Beryl Charlton
Introduction by Tony Hopkins
Designed and illustrated by Eric Dale
Maps by Ann Rooke
Photography by Eric Dale, Forestry Commission,
Simon Fraser, Jimmy Givens, Tony Hopper,
Northumbrian Water, Allan Potts and National
Park Staff.
The pictures of steam locomotives appearing on
pages 47 and 67 are reproduced by kind
permission of the R. W. Lynn Collection.
Typesetting by The Design Quarter, Newcastle.

Forest Enterprise

A contribution towards the production costs
of this publication has been made by Forest
Enterprise, the woodland management section of
the Forestry Commission.

ISBN 0 907632 270

Printed by Chatsworth Studios, Newcastle upon Tyne.

WALKS in Reiver Country

A guide to sixteen walks of between
3km (2 miles) and 20km (12¹/₂ miles) around
Hadrian's Wall, Kielder, Redesdale and North Tynedale

Northumberland
NATIONAL PARK

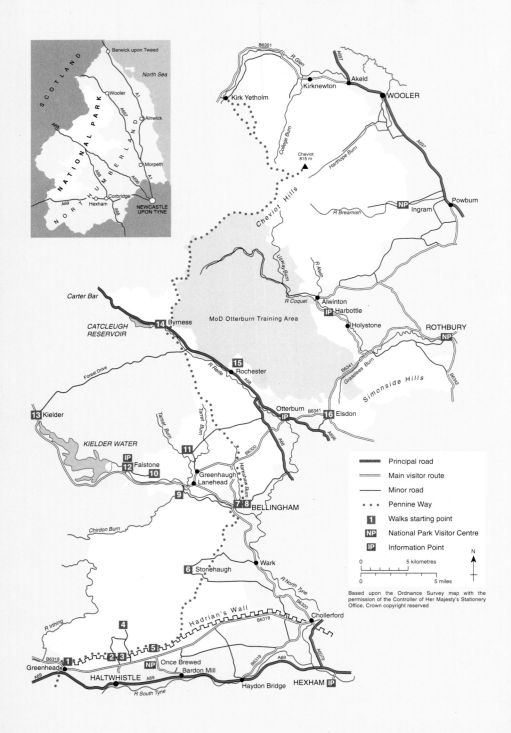

Contents

ENGLAND is a compact and congested country and it comes as a surprise to discover, on its northern border, an elemental landscape of wide horizons and lonely settlements.

Some of the most challenging walking country in Britain is to be found within Northumberland National Park; the Pennine Way, Hadrian's Wall and a host of old drove roads and ridge paths, famous or forgotten, lattice the hills and valleys.

For people who enjoy getting out into the countryside but appreciate accurate guidance and along-the-way information, this book gathers together some of the best and most interesting shorter walks in the southern half of the National Park, from Hadrian's Wall to Redesdale, and incorporates the Kielder area with its dramatic lake and forests.

This is the land of the infamous Border Reivers, families of thieves and rustlers who terrorised the region for 200 years and played a vital part in shaping the landscape and its legends.

Introduction

THE NATIONAL PARKS of England and Wales are unique in that they do not enshrine or preserve natural landscapes: they were created from farmed and managed land with a long history of settlement, unlike the 'Wilderness' Parks of the United States or the Game Parks of Africa. Britain's Parks are not state owned. The character or flavour of the countryside is so interwoven with traditional farming that it is hard to imagine what it would have looked like if it had not felt the cut of the plough or the footfall of a million sheep.

So, the 'wide blue yonder' of the National Park is not really wilderness at all and access should never be taken for granted. Rules of trespass apply as they do on any other private land, growing crops are easily damaged and the Ministry of Defence live firing ranges are closed to public access for most of the year. But in addition to its conservation aims the National Park Authority has a duty to encourage the provision of facilities for visitors. Footpaths are signposted, car parks and picnic sites maintained, access agreements are negotiated, and there are Visitor Centres and other outlets providing advice and information. This book is an example of team work within the National Park Authority, dealing with interpret-ation, conservation and rights of way and with the farming community, landowners and visitors.

In many ways these walks offer a cross section of the National Park and its essential features. There are traces of prehistoric settlement in a landscape more heavily populated in the Bronze Age than it is today, and the imprint of Roman rule, with the Wall and ruins of forts and townships. There's also the legacy of bleak border conflict as the land became a buffer between warring kingdoms, a wasteland or wilderness swept by the fear of reivers. For two centuries these rustlers and thieves terrorised the Borders. It was neighbour against neighbour, valley against valley rather than English against Scot and it marked one of the bloodiest chapters in Northumbrian history. It is less than four hundred years since the Union of the Crowns, less than half that time since farming began to flourish and make a mark on the land and only a few decades since the Ministry of Defence, the Forestry Commission and modern agriculture shaped the present system of land use.

Conservation of a whole landscape, an everyday working environment to farmers and foresters, is a difficult concept to put into practice. National Parks were established in the 1950s to conserve and enhance the natural beauty of outstanding upland areas of England and Wales amounting to one tenth of the land surface. Northumberland was the ninth to be designated, in 1956. The National Park Authority acts as a safeguard, a planning authority and an influence on agricultural and forestry developments. Within the Park farmers raise sheep and cattle, foresters crop timber, soldiers fight mock battles - and conservation officers and wardens talk to landowners, devise management agreements and try to keep the landscape alive and healthy. Within the National Park there are many Sites of Special Scientific Interest, two National Nature Reserves and a host of local Nature Reserves. Thus within a wide framework of landscape protection, the Park Authority encourages conservation whilst taking into account the essential economic and social roles of agriculture and forestry in the future of Northumberland.

National Park staff carrying out conservation work at Low Cleughs Bastle

A Special Place

NORTHUMBERLAND NATIONAL PARK covers 1030 square kilometres (398 square miles); it embraces the Cheviot massif, Simonside and the Harbottle Hills, Redesdale and Coquetdale, as well as the Wall and Tynedale areas covered in this book. The landscape of the Park is famous for its rolling hills and open moorland; the image in most people's minds is of silver skies awash with pale cobalt and oyster grey, and far horizons of ochre and magenta. This is only part of the picture, particularly towards the south of the Park where pastures and valleys soften the profile. The variety of details within a short walk in Tynedale is one of its most engaging features; a ridge of wind-swept heather or moor grass may be cut by a rocky cleft, leading down through a bower of hazel and oak and beside a tumbling burn, levelling out onto hay meadows and haughs. Drystone walls stand alongside blackthorn hedges, dour bastle houses overlook rose-decked cottages, distant singing may be a ring ouzel or a redstart.

Ring ouzel

The most important geological feature in the southern half of the National Park is the Whin Sill, an intrusion of hard volcanic rock pushed up between sediments of sandstone and limestone. The Sill's steep north face looks out over waves of grassland, pink and olive on the sandstone and emerald green where there are seams of limestone, then over shallow loughs and mires to Wark Forest. The south-facing dip slope of rush-covered pasture sweeps down by stages to the fertile Tyne Valley. Along the crest of the Whin Sill runs the Park's most important archaeological feature, Hadrian's Wall, a World Heritage Site and an attraction to thousands of visitors. Access is easy to all the most dramatic sections of the Wall, but finding circular walks in the immediate area is a problem. Those described in this book are certainly the pick of what is available, combining a clear archaeological theme with outstanding views of the Sill, the loughs and the far horizons of Cross Fell, the Cheviots and the Solway Coast.

Some of the most fascinating country-side in the Park lies a stone's throw to the north of the Whin ridge and several of the walks provide opportunities for exploring this forgotten corner, gaining a new perspective on the Wall's setting. Further north lies a matrix of forest and moor, a mecca for wildlife.

Wark Forest was established as part of the Forestry Commission's Kielder Forest in the 1950s and 1960s. At that time most of the planting consisted of blocks of Sitka spruce, but as these plantations have developed, so too have ideas about the role of forests in the countryside.

Today, Forest Enterprise, the manage-ment arm of the Forestry Commission, is committed to multi-purpose forestry, producing not only timber but also valuable wildlife habitats and recreational opportunities. The 62,000 hectares (153,000 acres) which make up the Kielder Forests are being re-planned and restructured so that as blocks of spruce are felled they are replaced by stands of different ages with more space and an increasing proportion of broadleaved trees.

Before Setting Off

EACH WALK begins with an accurate assessment of its length in kilometres and miles, a brief description of the terrain and an estimate of the time it is likely to take to complete, assuming a few distractions along the way. All the walks are circular varying in length from 3km (2 miles) to 20km (12½ miles). Two walks, 13 and 14 are strenuous. Families of moderate fitness should feel confident of attempting most routes with only a little preparation.

STARTING POINTS are from a suitable car parking space, either a formal parking area with a hard surface or a road verge wide enough to accommodate two or three cars at a time.

ALL ROUTES have been checked and signposts, stiles and waymarks provided where necessary. Occasionally a way-marking change in a section of the route may be met along the way. Unforseen but necessary alterations of this kind are carried out with as little inconvenience as possible to walkers.

THE ROUTE·SYMBOLS on the maps are as follows: Right of Way ▬▬▬▬
Permissive Path ▬ ▬ ▬ ▬ ▬

INTERPRETIVE NOTES are printed in the text in normal type, whilst route directions are given in bold type. GR refers to the Ordnance Survey grid reference system. Details on how to use this are printed on the 1:25,000 Pathfinder series of maps and on the 1:50,000 Landranger series. Sheets 80 and 87 (Landranger) cover all the walks in this publication.

COMFORT AND SAFETY are essential considerations when preparing for a walk. Heavy boots and woollen socks used to be the recommended footwear, but these days there are better alternatives. Go for something that is lightweight and fully waterproof, supports the ankle and has a non-slip sole. Carry a rucksack and pack a pullover or fleece and waterproof jacket.

The rucksack can be used for spare clothing, plasters, midge repellent and food. The pullover and waterproof are an acknowledgement that you are out on the hills; even in summer there can be a cold wind.

LOOK AFTER THE COUNTRYSIDE; it is in all our interests to do so. Walkers have a responsibility to leave the landscape as they found it and follow the Country Code. In particular, fasten all gates, keep to the recognised route and take any litter home. Most of the walks follow recognised foot-paths or bridleways but there are occasions when no rights of way exist and the path is by the permission of the land-owner or farmer. Please be considerate when passing houses or crossing farmland, leave machinery and livestock alone, and if you wish to take a dog, keep it under control.

Thirlwall Castle

Walltown Crags – Thirlwall Castle – Cairny Croft – Low Old Shield. 7km (4½ miles); about 2½ hours

A pleasant walk in the Wall area with spectacular views over contrasting landscapes. The route passes the ruins of one of Northumberland's most dramatic castles and follows a short stretch of the Tipalt Burn

It is an easy walk with one short, steep ascent. **Note:** Part of the route involves crossing the stepping stones at Cairny Croft. **Do Not** attempt this walk if water levels are high.

Turn north from the B6318 on unclassified road signed Roman Army Museum and Walltown Crags. Turn right opposite the entrance to the Roman Army Museum and follow the sign to Walltown Crags. Park in National Park car park about 400m (437 yards) beyond cattle grid (GR 674662).

Walk back down the road.

The mixed woodland on the left is planted mainly with oak and ash. In spring, the woodland floor is carpeted with bluebells and wood anemones.

In folklore, bluebells have always been associated with fairies. It was believed that if a child picked these flowers alone in a wood, he or she would never be seen again. Children today still play the old singing game "In and out of the dusky bluebells" unaware that it is a fairy song with a sinister meaning: "In and out of the dusky bluebells I am your master".

Cross the cattle grid, go through a wicket gate in the fence on the right and follow the footpath.

Conditions in the wild area bordering the edge of the path are just right for a host of summer-flowering plants. Betony, birdsfoot trefoil, herb robert, melancholy thistle, meadowsweet and rosebay willowherb grow in profusion and sweet, wild raspberries are there for eating.

Go up the steps and skirt Walltown Quarry. Follow the Pennine Way sign and meet the road near the quarry entrance.

1

Walltown Quarry was opened in 1871 employing 40 men and producing about 100 tons of whinstone a week, mainly for roadmaking. The quarry which destroyed an impressive section of Hadrian's Wall, closed in the early 1970s leaving an ugly scar on the landscape. A major reclamation scheme was undertaken by the National Park in the late 1980s to provide an attractive site for public enjoyment and recreation. Derelict buildings and machinery were removed, the area was infilled and landscaped, trees and shrubs planted and the quarry pond made into a lake.

Turn right along the road and just before the cattle grid cross over the stile on the left.

Here and down the hill as far as Thirlwall Castle the Wall ditch is in a good state of preservation. The ditch, which runs parallel to the Wall on its north side was intended to impede any attack from that direction. Although it was a standard Roman military ditch, V-shaped in section, the width and depth are not uniform throughout its length but on average it is 8m (27 feet) wide and 3m (9 feet) deep. The ditch was never continuous; it was only constructed in vulnerable places where the Wall had to come down from the crags.

Go downhill, keeping the Wall ditch on your left.

Ahead, on the valley floor, is the distinctive row of terraced houses at Longbyre. These are traditional brick-built pit cottages which once housed the families of miners working at the Baron Mine west of Greenhead.

Birdsfoot trefoil

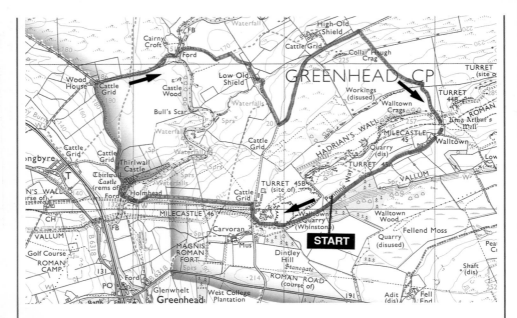

At the bottom of the hill, cross the stile and follow the zig-zag track down to the Tipalt Burn. Pause on the bridge.

The Tipalt Burn rises in Wark Forest and flows into the South Tyne near Haltwhistle. The picturesque hamlet of Thirlwall grew up around the castle whose dramatic ruins stand high above the steep west bank of the burn. The castle probably dates to the early 14th century when troubles with the Scots began in earnest. It is built entirely of stone robbed from the Roman Wall which ran nearby. The historian William Hutchinson who saw Thirlwall in 1776 described it as being "a dark and melancholy fortress, much in ruin". He commented on the thickness of the walls, up to 3m (9 feet) in places, and went on "The builder has even been afraid of the light, for the apertures are no larger than the stair-cases of ancient castles. The whole carries the appearance of a horrid gloomy dungeon, where its ancient tyrants dealt in deeds of darkness".

Continue on. After a short distance, leave the Pennine Way and follow the track as it curves round Thirlwall Castle.

On a sunny day it is hard to imagine that the castle has had a sinister past. Tradition has it that a dwarf guards a solid gold table at the bottom of a well somewhere inside the castle walls. There he remains under a mysterious

spell which no-one can remove except the only son of a widow. To this day, the well has never been discovered.

Go through the farmyard and continue uphill on the road taking the right fork for Wood House.

At the top of the hill there are good views in all directions. To the right are Walltown Crags and beyond them, to the north, Collar Heugh Crags. Ahead lies the barren expanse of Thirlwall Common, enclosed by Act of Parliament in 1801 and, in the distance, the forest.

Below, snaking along the valley floor and making use of the Tyne Gap, is the Newcastle to Carlisle railway, the first line to be built across Britain. The initial scheme put forward in the 1790s was for a canal linking the east and west coasts, but opposition from a number of landowners along the route was principally responsible for the withdrawal of the plan. By the early 1820s opinion had swung round in favour of a railway; an Act of Parliament was obtained in 1829, the first section of the line between Blaydon and Hexham was opened in 1835 and the remaining sections were completed in stages by 1839.

Turn right at the junction and follow the road as it descends to the Tipalt Burn just below Cairny Croft.

Cairny Croft is an early 19th century cottage which, until very recently, had no access other than on foot, no electricity and no water supply. The living quarters and stable were under one roof on single storey level and conditions generally for the occupants were, by late 20th century standards, very primitive.

At Cairny Croft leave the road at the fingerpost signed Low Old Shield and cross the burn via the stepping stones.

The exposed rock-face on the right-hand bend of the Tipalt Burn is a designated SSSI (Site of Special Scientific Interest) for its geological importance. This is the only limestone outcrop in the National Park which has been protected for its wealth of marine fossils.

On the far side of the burn turn left along the bank, go through the field gate, up the green track and follow the waymarkers to Low Old Shield. Go through the gate in the top left-hand corner of the field and through the farmyard. Follow the track round past the front of the house and up the hill. Pause to look back at Low Old Shield.

Cairny Croft from the Pennine Way

Low Old Shield

Low Old Shield, attractively situated by a tributary of the Tipalt Burn is a bastle, a 16th century defensible farmhouse, built as a temporary safe refuge against attacks by the Border Reivers. Bastle is most probably derived from the French word 'bastille' which means a strong place. Low Old Shield stands on a platform of massive boulders and the walls include many squared stones, recycled material from Hadrian's Wall! It is still a farmhouse although remodelled as a more conventional two-storeyed dwelling.

Continue up the farm track (ignoring the green track on the left), and turn left when you reach the tarmac road. Follow the road to the fingerpost on the right signed to Hadrian's Wall. Turn right here to cross the little footbridge and head uphill to the stile over the wall on the skyline. Cross the stile and follow the direction of the waymarkers over the field towards Walltown Crags.

The scalloped crest of the Whin Sill here used to be known as the Nine Nicks of Thirlwall, but quarrying in the past has so damaged the ridge that the name is no longer appropriate.

Go through the gateway, and follow the direction of the waymarker which will take you onto the Military Way.

The Military Way was the main Roman supply road for the garrisons along the Wall. It runs parallel with the Wall and is visible here as a green track, just below the ridge on the right.

Keeping the field wall on your left make your way down to the car park as it comes into view.

Mires and Molinia

2

Cawfields – Walltown – Low Tipalt. 8km (5 miles); about 2½ - 3 hours

A low level walk with the opportunity to see some different views of Hadrian's Wall. Gentle climbs using unclassified and very quiet roads. A stretch of fell land which can be wet underfoot, otherwise ground conditions are generally firm.

   This undulating countryside contains the best undamaged upland mires (peat bogs) in England, recognised nationally and internationally for the importance of their plant communities. Seven mires in the Wall area are wholly or partly protected as Nature Reserves and the National Park is actively involved in their management.

Roman remains at Great Chesters

even at that late date, but the intervening centuries have taken their toll and all that is left for today's visitor to marvel at are the vaulted underground strong-room, now ruinous, and the remains of the south gateway.

   The most remarkable feature about the fort was its aqueduct. Six miles long and stone-lined, it took water from the upper reaches of the Caw Burn to provide the garrison (500 men) with a running supply. It was an incredible feat of engineering which required only one bridge on its tortuous route. The course of the

Park at Cawfields picnic site (GR 713666). Leave the car park and, keeping the Caw Burn on your right, walk back down to the unclassified road. Turn right, across the bridge and go over the stone step stile on the left and into the field. Pass in front of Burnhead cottage.

Burnhead used to be a two up and two down cottage. It was last inhabited in 1939 by William Little, the foreman at Cawfields Quarry, his wife Sarah, their four children and two nephews. Thereafter it stood empty, except for storing hay during the winter, until 1991 when it was sold and modernised.

Continue on to Great Chesters, crossing two stiles and enter the area of the Roman fort by another stile.

The Romans called this fort Aesica. Built in AD128 it was one of three infantry forts (Housesteads and Birdoswald were the other two) along the Wall. William Stukeley, scholar and antiquarian, who visited Great Chesters in 1725 noted "Great marks of buildings all over it, and even side-walls of houses left". The remains must have been an impressive sight

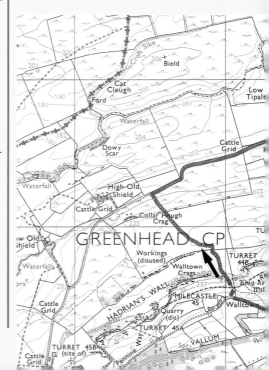

aqueduct, first traced by Dr. John Lingard in 1800, is plotted on O.S. maps of the area.

Turn left down the track to leave the fort by the south gateway.

It was here in 1894 that the Northumberland Excavation Committee discovered a superb hoard of Roman jewellery. The hoard included a silver enamelled brooch in the shape of a hare, a gold brooch, a bracelet, a neck pendant and two rings, one gold and one silver. Replicas of the jewellery hoard, the largest and most important ever found in Britain, are on display in the Museum of Antiquities in Newcastle.

Continue down the track.

The grass in the field to the right of the track will be turned into silage to provide winter fodder for Great Chesters farm. Ensilage is the process whereby crops are preserved in a green state. Silage is not a new venture. It is recorded that while on campaign in Gaul (France) Julius Caesar had silage made in pits lined with clay, to provide food for his horses during the winter months.

Silage-making in Britain didn't begin to develop until the 1920s; at that time the grass crop was stored in silos. It was the advent of black polythene making it easier to store silage in bags or in clamps in the ground, that eventually popularised the process.

At the end of the track, go through the gate and turn right along the tarmac road. Continue on and go through the next gate across the road.

On the right and running parallel to the road is a good stretch of the Vallum, the Roman earthwork marking the southern boundary of the military zone.

The farm on the crags to the right is named Cockmount Hill, 'cock' in this case meaning woodcock. There has been a settlement here for many centuries and the hillside is marked with the ridges and furrows of medieval ploughing.

At the junction for Cockmount Hill keep straight on, on a rough farm track and go through another gate.

On the left is Great Chesters Moss, one of the Border Mires. The wet acidic conditions are an ideal habitat for bog moss (Sphagnum), from which the local name for these mires, 'moss' is derived. The mire is like a huge peat sponge, at least 3m (9 feet) deep. It is home to an important variety of bog plants, including harestail cottongrass, sundew, butterwort and bog rosemary.

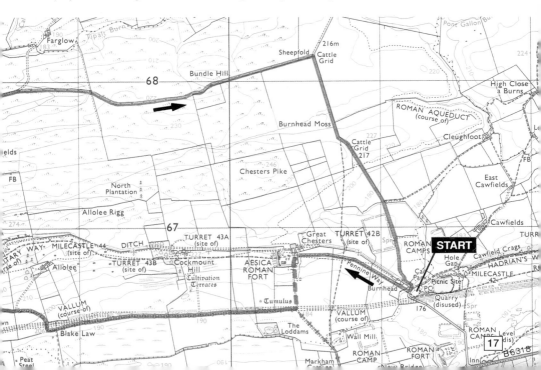

B6318

Bog rosemary is nationally rare but common in this area and westwards into Cumbria, where relatively mild winters and wet conditions have encouraged it to thrive. It grows on the drier cushions of peat and is often found in association with cranberry. It is related to the heather family and in summer has clusters of nodding pink flowers.

Bog rosemary

This sort of country is very difficult to negotiate; to cross it you need to know where the solid ground is. In the mid 17th century during the civil war between Parliament and Charles I a later generation of reivers took full advantage of the breakdown of central government to raid communities in the border area. To avoid detection on their forays, they used their knowledge of safe paths through the mosses and thus earned the feared name 'moss troopers'.

Follow the track as it bends to the right and cross the cattle grid.

On the right are the remains of a limekiln and behind it the exposed face of the limestone quarry. There are a number of limestone outcrops in the Wall area. The limestone was laid down about 300 million years ago when much of Northumberland was part of a warm, shallow sea. The rock was formed by the bodies of small aquatic creatures sinking to the sea bed where, over a long period of time they were compressed and fossilized.

Continue on towards Walltown.

In the reign of Edward VI Walltown was the seat and lordship of John Ridley, whose brother Nicholas Ridley, Bishop of London and Protestant martyr was burnt at the stake alongside Bishop Latimer in 1555 in the reign

of Bloody Mary. John Ridley lived in a castellated tower slightly to the north-west of the present farmhouse; the outlines show up beneath the grass. The tower was in ruins by the mid 18th century when George Marshall Esq built his farmhouse from the stone. George Marshall was "eminently beloved by his tenants, and the whole neighbourhood, for letting his lands at moderate rents". The old village of Walltown, which lay south of the farmhouse, has long since disappeared.

Just before you reach Walltown, turn right beside the stone troughs and follow the farm track.

Near the bottom of the track on the left, beside the troughs, are some large blocks of Roman masonry. These have been robbed from the milecastle (no.45) at the top of the hill at some time in the past.

Head uphill on the track to Walltown Nick.

In the middle of the gap, is King Arthur's Well. King Arthur is connected by legend with the area. The well is now topped with a man-hole cover. According to tradition, Paulinus baptised King Egbert (or King Edwin) and several hundred of his followers, here in AD 627 but the story has no real basis in fact. The well is a natural spring which provides water for Walltown Farm.

Walltown Nick is one of nine nicks or gaps along the Whin Sill. They were weak places in the band of hard rock which were scoured out by melting water under the ice sheet during the last Ice Age, to make the gaps you see today.

Walltown Farm

The Whin Sill has been designated an SSSI (Site of Special Scientific Interest) for the rich species of herbs that grow there, including common rock-rose, wild thyme and chives. Wild chives, thin grey-green spiky plants, grow among the rocky outcrops. William Camden, the 16th century historian who visited the Wall in Elizabeth I's reign wrote that "The Roman soldiers of the marches did plant here every where in old time for their use, certain medicinable hearbs, for to cure wounds: whence is it that some Emperick practitioners of Chirurgy in Scotland, flock hither every yeare in the beginning of summer, to gather such simples and wound herbes; the vertue whereof they highly commend as found by long experience and to be of singular efficacy". It is said that the chives were introduced by the Romans.

Keep straight on along the track. Go through the gateway in the stone wall and fork left to follow the direction of the waymarkers over a rise to a stile in the stone wall ahead.

Look back from here at the more rarely seen north face of the Whin Sill with the Wall riding high on top. Local rumour has it that the folk living on the north side of the Wall have a month less summertime than those on the south side. At a glance you can see why. It is wide, open, seemingly barren country with acres of land and sky.

Cross the stile, go downhill and over the footbridge at the bottom to the tarmac

The north face of the Whin Sill

road. Turn right and continue on towards Low Tipalt.

Just past the cattle grid and over to the right is another Border Mire, Hangingshields Moss. Cross-leaved heath and bog asphodel can be found here, as well as insects such as the Manchester treble-bar moth and the large heath butterfly.

Bog asphodel

Pass Low Tipalt.

The fenced-off area to the right is the site of a National Park conservation project carried out in partnership with the farmer at Low Tipalt. The ground is wet and badly drained; it has little feeding value for livestock but it will provide support for certain trees. Birch and alder have been planted to form a scrub woodland and marsh which will provide a mixed wildlife habitat.

Leave the road as it bends left and follow the route shown by the bridleway signpost on the right.

The predominant vegetation here is Molinia, purple moor grass, an acidic-loving plant which used to form huge areas of prairie in the peat uplands. This was the landscape chosen by the Forestry Commission in the mid 1920s for the planting of conifers; thus Kielder Forest has been responsible for the demise of the great Northumbrian prairies.

Continue on and make for the metal field gate ahead. Go through the gate, bear right and follow the direction of the waymarker across the next fell.

The derelict house down to the left, standing on the bank of the Tipalt Burn, is High Tipalt. The outbye farms seem pleasantly secluded on a summer's day but their bleak remoteness in winter can only be imagined. Indeed, 300 years ago these places were only grazed in summer when shepherds lived in temporary summer accommodation called shielings. By the late 18th century many had become permanent settlements and took their name from this traditional practice of shieling, for instance High Old Shield, Low Old Shield and Shield on the Wall.

Head for the corner of the field wall and, with the wall on your right, continue on until you reach a farm gate. Go through the gate and pause at the top of the rise.

The views north and east are expansive. Eastwards, your eye is drawn along the Whin Sill towards Sewingshields Crag and the wave-like landscape beyond. The steep north-facing scarp of the Whin Sill casts dark shadows on the fields below. To the north lies Wark Forest and mile after mile of conifer plantation which is part of the great enterprise of Kielder.

Still keeping the wall on your right continue on to the next gate.

Field vole

This open ground is an ideal habitat for field voles, the chief prey of short-eared owls which frequently hunt by day. They are by far the best mousetrap a farmer can have on his land, especially in years when there is a plague of rodents. The short-eared owl may lay up to four eggs. The eggs are incubated as soon as they are laid, so the first laid is the first to hatch. The owlet is therefore bigger than the rest. If there is a food shortage it has a better chance of survival because the parents will feed it and let the younger ones starve, an excellent example of investing resources wisely. As the younger ones grow weaker, they may even be ripped up by the parents and fed to the bigger owlets.

20

Go through the gate, across the field and turn right onto the road.

As you walk along the road you may notice the marked difference between the improved fields on either side and the open fell and bog to the north. Trees which once covered the landscape here, as elsewhere, are now conspicuous by their absence, except in small shelter belts, usually next to farm steadings.

Land enclosure and land improvement came very late to this part of the country (late 18th century) and many of the drystone walls date back to this time. The walls are mainly sandstone and are an important feature in this landscape. On any farm there are hundreds of yards of wall, which are costly and difficult to maintain. Cheaper alternatives are often employed, such as post and wire fencing.

Drystone walling

Continue on, over the cattle grid and down the hill. Follow the road past Burnhead, across the bridge and turn left back to Cawfields car park.

The Caw Burn at Cawfields picnic site

Hadrian's Wall and Wade's Road

3

Cawfields - Caw Gap - Hallpeat Moss. 6km (4 miles); about 2 hours

A walk over rolling country with expansive views in all directions. The first part of the route includes a stretch of Hadrian`s Wall with good examples of a milecastle and a turret. Generally dry underfoot with one or two muddy sections and a couple of short but steep ascents.

Park at Cawfields Quarry picnic site (GR 713666) reached by the minor road signed Whiteside which leads north from the Milecastle Inn on the Military Road (B6318).

Cawfields was once an active working quarry. The dolerite (whinstone) of the Whin Sill was originally used to make stone sets for the roadways of the industrial towns and cities of the north. The sets were dressed on site and transported by narrow gauge railway down the Haltwhistle Burn to the storage facilities at Townend. Until 1955 the quarry was providing whinstone chippings for tarmac roads which replaced the stone sets.

The old quarry was eventually acquired by Northumberland National Park in 1972 and has been landscaped with a car park and picnic facility. The lake which has replaced the quarry pond is cold and deep and too dangerous for swimming to be allowed.

Leave the car park by the path to the left of the lake.

The quarry face at the east end of the site clearly shows the formation of the strata produced by a volcanic intrusion. The solidified columns are typical of this fine-grained rock.

Go through the kissing gate, turn right, walk uphill and through the kissing gate in the fence across Hole Gap. Turn left and head for the milecastle.

To make identification easier, all forts, milecastles and turrets along the line of Hadrian's Wall are numbered from east to west. This milecastle is number 42. It was built here to

protect Hole Gap, one of several weak places in the Roman frontier defences where the Wall has to come down from the crags.

The steep slope of the bedrock here must have made this milecastle an uncomfortable post to man.

Milecastle 42, Cawfields

Keeping the Wall on your left, continue on.

Rowan and aspen grow naturally on the scarp, the steep cliff face on the north side of the Wall. Aspen is less common now in Britain than it used to be. It is often called `the whispering tree' from the noise the leaves make when the slightest breeze blows through them. In autumn, the changing colours of the foliage and the red berries of the rowan bring an added beauty to the Whin Sill crags.

Follow the Wall as it dips down at Thorny Doors.

For a long time this part of the Wall was the highest visible section, until later excavations uncovered a higher stretch on the east side of Sycamore Gap, and more recently at the site of Milecastle 37, near Housesteads.

Continue on and stop at the top of the next rise.

This is the highest point on the walk and worth pausing to take in the air and the views. To the south is the gentle and sheltered valley of the South Tyne, with the North Pennines beyond. By contrast, the country north of the Wall is wilder and more open, dotted with small farmsteads and backing onto the seemingly endless Wark Forest. In the distance, rising from the trees is the early warning mast of Hopealone.

The forest extends continuously to Kielder and beyond. The farming value of much of this land is poor and forestry was considered an attractive economical alternative. To the east and west are classic Hadrian's Wall views with rippling bands of sandstone and limestone dipping away to the horizon like petrified waves.

Continue alongside the Wall to Turret 41a.

This turret shows some of the rethinking that took place during the design and construction of the Wall. The initial plan was for a wall 3m (10 feet) wide and its foundations can be seen on the north side of the turret. But at a later stage, for whatever reason, cheapness or speed of construction or both, the plans were changed and a 2.5m (8 feet) wide wall was built on top of the original wider foundations.

Towards the end of the second century, following a serious rebellion by a local tribe, the Brigantes, there was a further change in the defence plan and the turret was considered obsolete. It was dismantled and the Wall was rebuilt across the site.

Descend with the Wall to the kissing gate at Caw Gap.

Throughout its length the Wall was protected on the north by a ditch, except where the Whin Sill made this unnecessary. One of the best preserved stretches of the ditch can be seen here on the west side of Caw Gap.

Go through the gate, turn right onto the road then left over a ladder stile and follow the fingerpost signed Military Road downhill to the Vallum.

The Vallum is a ditch with a mound on either side. It was part of the Roman frontier system and runs south of and parallel to the Wall, except where there are forts and it has to make a detour. This earthwork was a clearly recognisable boundary to warn civilians that they were approaching the military zone.

Cross the Vallum and make for the left-hand corner of the field wall ahead.

You are now walking through improved pasture which in summer contrasts markedly with the rough grassland on the south-facing slope of the Whin Sill. The grasses on the drier areas at the top give way to rushes in the wetter areas at the bottom.

The improved pasture is heavily grazed. In the summer months the cowpats attract dung flies which lay their eggs in these highly nutritious deposits.

Continue on to the Military Road.

The road runs from Carlisle to Newcastle but the only connection it has with the Romans is that in places it is built on top of the flattened remains of Hadrian's Wall. At a crucial stage in the 1745 Jacobite rebellion, General Wade commanding George II's forces and stationed at Newcastle was unable to get his artillery across to Carlisle to halt Bonnie Prince Charlie's march south, as there wasn't a decent road. After the rebellion was suppressed it was decided to build a new road between Newcastle and Carlisle, the narrowest part of the country and therefore the fastest route for dealing with any future Jacobite uprising. Despite protests from antiquarians, the work went ahead and since then the road has been

View east to Shield on the Wall from Cawfields Crag

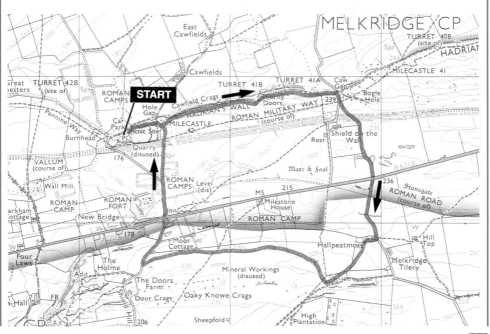

The Military Road

Climb over the stile, cross the road and continue along the minor road ahead signed Melkridge until you reach Hallpeat Moss Farm on the right. Pass the garden wall and cross over the ladder stile into the meadow.

There are two theories about how Hallpeat Moss got its name. One is that it was the place where peat was cut for the Hall, the hall being Willimoteswyke, inhabited by the Ridleys who owned most of the land round here. The second is that it is the house next to the peat moss (peat bog).

The architectural style of the house is quite unusual. Built as a linear farm with the byres on the first floor level, Hallpeat Moss is more reminiscent of architectural styles in the North Pennines than it is typical of the square-set arrangement of farm buildings in this area. The stone-flagged roof is becoming a rare sight on old farmhouses in Northumberland.

Make for the bottom left-hand corner of the meadow. Cross the stile, cut the corner of the next field and go through the squeeze stile. Turn right and follow the ill-defined path running parallel to the field wall.

The ground on the left shows considerable signs of disturbance. There used to be an old

called Wade's Road or the Military Road. It is now a tourist route but traffic can be very fast so take care when you cross.

drift mine here owned by the Blackett-Ords, one of the great coal-mining families in the north. It was worked commercially in the 1870s, employing many men and pit ponies. The entrance remained open long after the mine closed and was eventually sealed when the mine became unsafe.

Go through the kissing gate on the right and head towards the trees on the skyline. Continue uphill for about 180m (165 yards) until you reach a broad grassy track. Turn left and keeping the field wall on your right, follow the track along the ridge.

The land on either side of the track is pock-marked with large, circular depressions; these are the silted-up remains of shallow coal workings. By the late 18th century, farmers were beginning to exploit local outcrops of coal to fuel lime kilns. The kilns were filled with alternate layers of coal and limestone, the coal was set alight and the resulting burnt lime was spread on the land to improve the quality of the grass for grazing. The ridge also bears the scars of extensive quarrying for limestone.

Where the track divides, take the left fork and continue downhill. Cross the ladder stile by the gate and turn right onto the road.

This minor road is called the Shield Hill and climbs steeply up from Haltwhistle to join the Military Road. The name Shield is derived from 'shieling' the practice in upland areas of driving cattle and sheep to graze the higher pastures in summer.

Walk down the road.

To the left, the Haltwhistle burn cuts its way through a narrow, steep-sided valley. At the turn of the century the valley was a hive of commercial activity, with brick works, coal mines and a waggonway from Cawfields quarry to Haltwhistle. The industrial enterprise has long since gone and the valley is now a popular wooded walk.

Artist's impresson of
a limekiln in operation,
mid 19th century.
Illustration: Ric Scollins

Continue on to the crossroads by the Milecastle Inn.

The Milecastle Inn used to be called the Common House, probably because it was near the common, but to many locals it is still the North Jerry. Jerry was short for Jerry-shop which in 19th century local terminology meant a public house. There was a South Jerry, the Sportsmans' Inn at Coanwood, near Haltwhistle. When this closed, the locals transferred their custom to the Wallace Arms at Featherstone and this in turn became the South Jerry.

Cross the Military Road carefully. Continue along the minor road signed Whiteside as far as the bend, then take the path signed Milecastle 42 across the field to the right.

To the right of the path are the sites of two Roman temporary camps, possibly used to accommodate the men who were building the Wall.

Follow the path back to Hole Gap and return to the car park.

Scotchcoulthard – Hindleysteel – Hopealone.
8km (5 miles); about 2½ hours

4

Not so very long ago large areas of upland Britain were smothered by conifers. Now all that has changed. As mature trees from the first planting are felled, forests are being restructured to provide greater diversity. With their enormous variety of wildlife and the feeling of peace and quiet that wood-lands always seems to have, they are much more interesting and attractive than they used to be.

This route provides a glimpse of a landscape which is changing for the better. The going is easy, on good tracks and forest roads all the way.

If you are approaching by car, turn north off the B6318 (Military Road), 3km (2 miles) south-west of the National Park Centre at Once Brewed to follow the unclassified road signposted Edges Green. Continue over the cattle grid past Edges Green and on to the forest. After reaching the edge of the forest continue straight ahead past two forest roads on the right and the access road to Scotchcoultard on the left. Park beside the track (GR 724712) taking care not to obstruct the gateway.

Go over the stile by the gate and down the track.

You have now entered the southern edge of Wark Forest which is part of the larger forest of Kielder. This used to be Henshaw Common but it is now completely planted over, apart from one small area centred round Hummell Knowe to the left, the last remaining piece of common land in the Wall area still grazed by commoners.

Common land is a legacy of the time when much of the English countryside was wild,

ownerless and used in common. After the Norman Conquest the Lord of the Manor became the legal owner but the peasants continued to have some rights, such as free grazing for their animals and wood for fires. By the mid 19th century most of the common land had been enclosed for improvement by a new breed of agricultural entrepreneurs, landlords who were prepared to invest in the land and farmers who had the money and the skills to introduce new methods of farming. Today there are less than 554,850 hectares (1½ million acres) of common land in England.

Follow the track until it bends round to the right.

From here you can see how the restructuring programme for Wark Forest is progressing. The first crop of trees planted in the 1940s and 50s has been clear-felled and the harvested timber taken out. The new crop has a greater mix of trees, planted as much for ecological benefit and aesthetic appearance as for commercial production. The restructuring includes planting a large number of native Scots pine instead of Sitka and Norway spruce, the dominant trees in the original scheme.

For the first few years, these new plantations will lead to a dramatic increase in the number of voles and mice, the main food source of predatory birds and foxes. On winter days, short-eared owls can be seen quartering the area, but when the trees have developed sufficiently to hide the ground cover then the hunters will be forced to look elsewhere.

Continue on through an old gateway and into the mature forest.

Horsetail ferns grow in the wetter areas at the foot of the ruinous drystone wall on the right. During the Carboniferous period 300 million years ago when this part of the country was covered by tropical forest (hard to believe!) these ferns grew to the size of trees. The most distinctive part of the plant is the stem and its fossilised remains can sometimes be found in the coals, shales and sandstones in the Wall area.

In today's much colder climate, common horsetail grows to less than a metre (3 feet) in height. With its deep, penetrating root system and its ease of reproduction – one small fragment of root will produce a whole new plant – horsetail is a gardener's nightmare!

Keep on to Tod Sike and either jump across or cross by the footbridge just to the right.

Whilst most people are familiar with the derivation of Tod, the Anglo-Saxon word for fox, the origin of Sike is less well-known. In fact

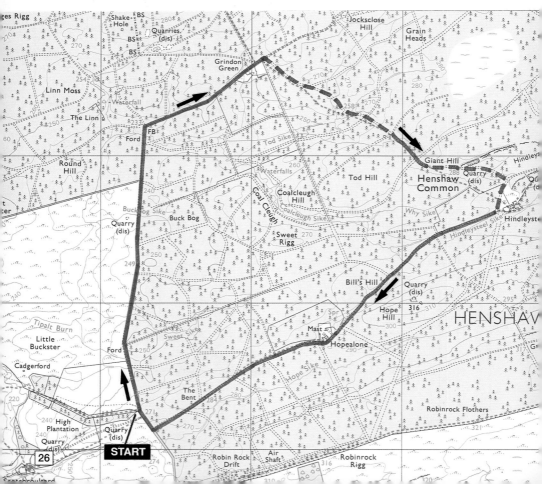

Roe deer

After a short distance join the forest road and almost immediately take the next turning on the right. Pass between the gate posts and keep straight on.

Conifer forests are deceptively quiet places but many creatures live there without disturbing the stillness. Forest edges provide a good living for rabbits and foxes. In winter months, large flocks of crossbills descend on the treetops to feed on the rich harvest of seeds. Crossbills have a specially adapted beak for this. They use the crossed tips to prise open the scales of cones then twist out the seeds. The adult male crossbill is bright crimson in colour, the female yellow-green.

The broader verges along the road have been invaded by creeping thistle. Regarded as a pest on agricultural land, in the forest it is allowed to flourish. The purple flower heads are a valuable source of nectar for numerous insects such as hover flies and ladybirds, and butterflies like the small tortoiseshell and painted lady.

Coltsfoot grows in the barren, stony ground on the roadside. It is one of the earliest spring flowers with the stems and yellow heads appearing before the leaves. The shape of the leaves, like a colt's foot, has given the plant its name. In summer and late autumn, long after the flowers have died, coltsfoot can still be recognised by the leaves which sometimes reach the size of dinner plates!

Coltsfoot

it is a Northumbrian word for a narrow water course and a glance at any map of the county will show how widespread the name and feature are.

In early morning, at dusk and sometimes during the day, the glade to the right is frequented by roe deer. Native to Britain, these shy, rather solitary animals were almost wiped out by hunting. They are very wary of people, so you need a certain amount of luck to see one. Being quiet and downwind are distinct advantages. Although their eyesight is poor their sense of hearing and smell is extremely acute. If you stand still they may not see you clearly, but when they do they will run for cover.

Continue along the track forking right between the conifers until you reach a cleared area on the right.

This was the site of Grindon Green, one of several small outbye farms north of the Wall worked in the early 1930s. Engulfed by stiff stands of conifers, all that now remains of Grindon are the derelict drystone wall and the enclosed inbye fields around the farmstead which have been planted up with broadleaves.

Upland areas were particularly hard-hit by the depression of the 1930s. Most outlying farms were making a very poor living so when the Forestry Commission offered to buy Grindon and its land, rehouse the occupants in one of the new forestry villages and provide regular, paid employment the offer was too good to turn down. Some farmers who didn't want to give up their farms became the victims of compulsory purchase orders. By these means the Forestry Commission acquired the vast area of land which is now Kielder Forest.

Follow the track as it bends round to the right.

Hindleysteel is in the clearing on the left. The buildings and small field are all that remains of another small outbye farm taken over by the Forestry Commission.

Hopealone mast appears on the right.

The mast was erected in the early 1950s as part of Britain's early warning system. This was before the National Park was designated. Had the application for this structure been made now, it would have been rejected by the Park's strict planning controls on the grounds that it represents an intrusion in the landscape. Although the mast is an eyesore and can be seen for miles around, the steel girders have provided a perfect nesting site for a pair of kestrels, the county's most adaptable raptor.

Continue on to where the forest road becomes a tarmac road. This is the highest point of the walk.

From here there are extensive views to the west and north. Looking ahead, (due west), you can see the wild landscape of the Bewcastle Fells and the cleft of the Irthing Valley; to the right (due north) is the dark expanse of Kielder Forest which disappears over the horizon to the Scottish border.

Follow the tarmac road and at the junction turn right, walk past the access road to Scotchcoulthard and journey's end.

If any place in this bleak landscape deserves to be haunted it is Scotchcoulthard. This wasteland was one of the escape routes for the

notorious Border Reivers who raided Tynedale in the 16th century. Some didn't make it to the safety of this wild land. The deep and dangerous peat bogs made it a hazardous place to venture and only the reivers knew the safe paths.

Many a reiver made his last stand at Scotchcoulthard facing the fury of the Tynedale men who had been robbed of their cattle and possessions. Human remains and weapons found in the area when the forest was planted suggest that fighting took place here. It is recorded that Hobie Noble, a reiver of repute, was betrayed at Scotchcoulthard, taken prisoner and later hanged at Carlisle Castle.

Steel Rigg – Rapishaw Gap – Greenlee – Gibbs Hill.
12km (7½ miles); 5 hours

A World Heritage Site and a National Nature Reserve feature in this exhilarating walk.

The first leg follows the Pennine Way National Trail eastwards along Hadrian's Wall to Rapishaw Gap then north across Ridley Common. The route turns west, skirting Greenlee Lough and the edge of Wark Forest to Gibbs Hill and back to Steel Rigg.

A fairly strenuous beginning followed by an easier stretch over grassland and farm tracks, muddy in places. The final section with one long, gradual ascent, is on tarmac road.

Park at Steel Rigg car park (GR 751677) 1km north of the National Park Centre at Once Brewed on the B6318.

Leave the car park by the kissing gate. Walk down the side of the paddock, go through the wicket gate on the left and follow the path along the north side of Hadrian's Wall to the corner.

The view looking east is one of the most breathtaking in England. The landscape is dominated by the Whin Sill crags, stretching away as far as the eye can see. Immediately ahead is the grim, grey face of Peel Crags, a popular climbing pitch with Crag Lough beyond.

Hadrian's Wall was designated a World Heritage site in 1987. The length on the right was excavated and reconstructed by the 19th century antiquarian John Clayton. During his lifetime, Clayton acquired several miles of the Wall and a number of forts, including Chesters where he lived. Here at Peel Gap, he used Roman stone to reface the original core and turf to provide a walkway on the top. At the time this was probably a good idea but the many thousands of visitors who have walked along the Wall since have destroyed the turf, leaving the stonework unprotected.

Continue downhill to Peel Gap.

The stone slabs forming the footpath across Peel Gap were laid by the National Park field staff, to allow the vegetation to recover in an area made bare and boggy by the passing of many feet. Similar schemes of maintenance have been carried out on other heavily worn sections of the path.

The Roman remains in Peel Gap were excavated during the 1980s by archaeologists working for the National Trust which owns much of the land in the central area of the Wall. The stones here are in their original position and the Wall has been consolidated using modern cement. The culverts, put in when the Wall was built, allow the surface water to drain away.

Another interesting feature is the turret, not built as part of the Wall but butted up against it at a later date. The turret was added to strengthen this weak place in the frontier defences.

Climb up to the top of Peel Crags.

The view on a clear day is well worth the effort of the climb. To the west is Winshields Crag, at 345m (1132 feet) the highest point on the Wall. Cross Fell and Cold Fell lie to the south-west. The heather-clad hill due south is Barcombe Fell where the Romans quarried stone for the Wall and its defences; behind Barcombe are the Allendale Fells. If the visibility is good you should be able to pick out some of the flue chimneys built during the early 19th century to carry the poisonous gases away from the lead smelting which operated there.

Peel Crags and Crag Lough from Steel Rigg

5

29

Mallard drake

With the Wall on your left, continue along the crags, past the site of turret 39a and cross the ladder stile at the bottom of Cat Stairs.

Cat Stairs got its name from the jumble of stones which fell from the Wall as it gradually deteriorated. It was believed that only a cat was nimble enough to climb up this stretch.

In the 18th century local farmers took stone from the Wall to build farmhouses, byres, barns and field walls.

Continue on to Castle Nick, named after Milecastle 39 which occupies the gap.

Milecastle 39 was uncovered in 1854 by John Clayton. It was built to accommodate about 20 men whose duty was to patrol the Wall and look out for any threats from the north. Gates to the north and south allowed soldiers and civilians to pass through. Excavation between 1985 and 1987 showed that Milecastle 39 was occupied until the late fourth century and beyond; the stone building in the north-west corner was an 18th century milking parlour!

Milecastle 39, Castle Nick

Climb to the top of the next crags.

The rectangular buildings against the base of the Wall are the remains of shielings. These temporary shelters were used in times past by shepherds and stockmen, whose sheep and cattle grazed the common land north of the Wall in the summer months. The shielings were built of Roman stone and may have been thatched with either heather or rushes.

Follow the path down into Sycamore Gap.

This place achieved fame in the early 1990s when it was used as one of the locations for the film Robin Hood, Prince of Thieves. The lone sycamore is reaching the end of its lifespan and the sapling planted nearby will ensure that the name Sycamore Gap will continue.

At Sycamore Gap cross the Wall and follow the stone-pitched path which leads to the top of Highshield Crags.

The path was laid to divert walkers away from the Wall where the foundations had been damaged by persistent trampling. Work was carried out in the summer of 1992 by National Park Wardens and field staff and by volunteers from the National Trust.

The stone flags came from the floors of disused cotton mills in Lancashire. Because of the difficulty of access, the stones had to be airlifted in by helicopter to prevent damage to the unique flora that grows on this area of the Whin Sill.

Much information about Roman bonding materials has come to light during consolidation work on this section of the Wall. The original mortar was puddled clay but when large-scale rebuilding took place at the end of the second century, proper mortar – lime, sand and water – was used. The mortar has lasted for eighteen centuries and efforts have been made to discover the reason for this. Analysis has proved that the secret ingredient in the mix was 60% animal fat. The builders of the Wall would have required hundreds of carcasses; imagine the stench this process would have made!

Cross the ladder stile ahead. The path runs close to the edge of the crags so take care!

From here there's an excellent view of Crag Lough below. Thousands of years ago during the last Ice Age, the lough was a shallow depression scoured out of the bedrock by the movement of an ice sheet. When the ice retreated, meltwater filled the depression, forming a lake. Mute swans are usually on the water; there are other wildfowl – moorhen, coot and mallard – but you need binoculars to see them clearly from this height. When John Clayton owned this lough it contained pike, roach, trout, perch and eels.

From Highshield Crags descend through the woodland, cross three ladder stiles and with the Wall now on your left, follow the path round to Milecastle 38, Hotbank.

An inscribed slab now in the Museum of Antiquities in Newcastle, records that this milecastle was built by the Second Augusta legion when Aulus Platorius Nepos was governor of Britain between AD122 – 126. Milecastle 38 was excavated in 1935.

Hotbank Farm to the left is owned by the National Trust. It is a fine example of a traditional Northumbrian farm steading; its character has not been spoilt by the addition of modern sheds. Hotbank is an unusually large farm for this area; 405 hectares (1000 acres) and all of it farmed by one family.

Keep on and at the top Hotbank Crags, pause to recover your breath.

Looking north you can see the layout of a typical hill farm, with the improved pasture, inbye, around the farmstead and the rough pasture, outbye, beyond. The weather for most of the year is cold and wet and the only crop the farmer can grow successfully is grass. This is made into either hay or silage for winter fodder. Four loughs are visible from here; Crag Lough to the west, Greenlee to the north, Broomlee to the north-east and Grindon to the south-east.

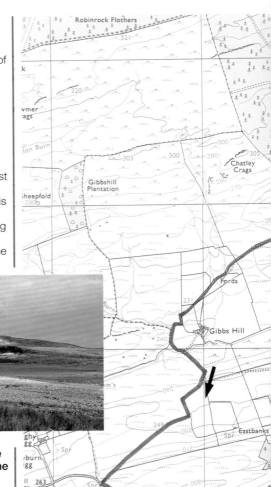

Broomlee Lough

Carry on to Rapishaw Gap. Cross over the ladder stile on your left and continue on the Pennine Way to the next stile.

The Pennine Way was Britain's very first long distance footpath, a 'long green trail' conceived in 1935 by Tom Stephenson. It took 30 years to gain ministerial approval and to negotiate new paths to provide a continuous route. The trail is a 400km (250 miles) high hills walk along the backbone of England. It starts at Edale in Derbyshire and finishes at Kirk Yetholm in southern Scotland. It is estimated that more than 7,000 people walk the full length of the Pennine Way every year. Many more tackle short sections over days or weekends.

North of the Wall, the way follows an old cart track across Ridley Common. The track was laid in the early 19th century to limestone quarries and kilns in the area.

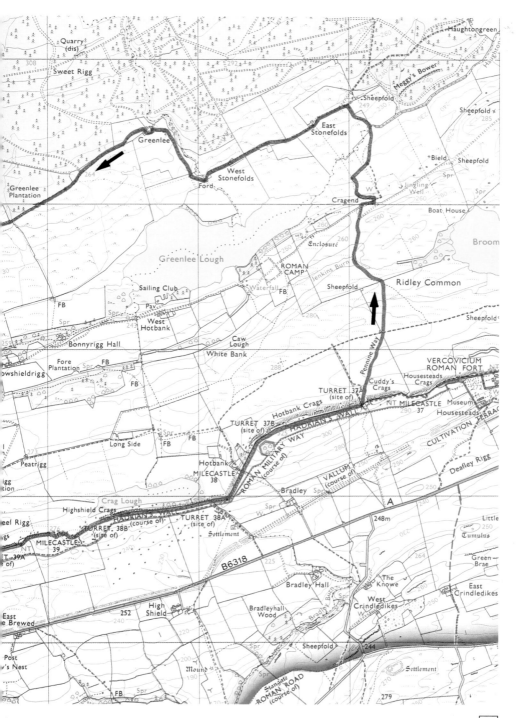

Cross the ladder stile and continue on the well-defined track, passing a recent limestone quarry on the right-hand side.

Broomlee Lough to the right is another shallow lake left in a glacial basin after the last Ice Age. Above the lough, towers Sewingshields Crags part of the Great Whin Sill. Here the ridge of the Whin Sill turns due south for a short stretch before reverting to its west-east alignment at Busy Gap.

Cross the next ladder stile and follow the track downhill to the burn.

The area you are crossing is an SSSI (Site of Special Scientific Interest) by English Nature, for the flora and fauna found in the wet flushes and burns which drain the land. Plants include white-flowered grass of Parnassus, a variety of sedges and the northern marsh orchid.

Cross the burn and continue on.

At this point there is a noticeable change in the vegetation cover, from grass to heather. This indicates a change in the underlying rock from limestone and shale to sandstone. Sandstone produces a dry, more acidic soil, ideal growing conditions for heather. At one time these heather-clad fells would have been managed as grouse moors; now they are grazed by sheep. In spring, you may be lucky enough to see or hear one of the red grouse that still nest in this area.

Grouse nest

Ahead and to the right are Queens Crags with their crown of heather. Below Queens Crags is the Rabbit Stone, so-called because it looks like a pair of rabbit's ears sticking up out of the heather.

At the field gate cross the step stile by fingerpost signed Pennine Way. Follow the track to the right hand then turn sharp left downhill. At the bottom turn right to the footbridge.

The stretch of water to the left is Greenlee Lough, bought by the National Park Authority in 1991. The dark line on the north shore is a band of peat exposed by waves washing away the soft bankside.

Go over the footbridge and turn right. Follow the Pennine Way waymarker to the top of the rise. Go downhill to cross the stile over the drystone wall. Cross the footbridge. Go uphill half left to the end of the wall. Climb over the ladder stile by the fingerpost signed Gibbs Hill. Turn left along the farm track.

To the right of the track is the southern edge of Wark Forest. Much of the area has been clear-felled. Replanting includes hardwoods and Scots pine, native species that blend into the landscape and will improve the look of the forest when it grows, particularly when viewed from Hadrian's Wall.

At East Stonefolds, cross the step stile and follow the track to the left of the house and outbuildings. Climb over the ladder stile and continue on to West Stonefolds. Go through the field gate, pass in front of the house and cross the ladder stile.

West Stonefolds, a small outbye farm bought many years ago by the Forestry Commission. was rescued from dereliction and is privately owned. The drystone wall by the ladder stile and the two small shelterbelts on either side of the property have been grant-aided by the National Park as a conservation project.

Turn left and continue along the track to the ford at Greenlee Burn. Cross the burn and the ladder stile, and go straight on.

You are now on Greenlee Farm. The land was acquired by Northumberland National Park in the early 1970s to prevent the extension of the forest down to the north shore of Greenlee Lough.

Greenlee, the largest of the Roman Wall loughs, extends to over 42 hectares (105 acres) and is a designated National Nature Reserve. Of particular value are the reed beds which provide cover for a number of summer visitors including reed bunting and sedge warbler. During the winter months Greenlee supports wildfowl such as wigeon, goldeneye, teal and whooper swan.

Greenlee Lough

At the waymarker turn right and follow the farm track to the ladder stile. Cross the stile and head uphill to Greenlee Farm. At the farm gate turn left and then right at the corner of the garden wall. Cross the ladder stile, go through the field gate and turn left along the farm track.

From the track there are excellent views south over Greenlee Lough towards the north face of Highshields Crags, with the Wall running along the top. Beyond are the Allendale Fells in the North Pennines.

Continue along the track. Cross over the next two ladder stiles and keep straight on.

This land is part of Gibbs Hill Farm. Due to changes in agricultural policy, the Government has set up the Countryside Stewardship Scheme by which farmers are paid to reduce the number of sheep and cattle on the farm and manage the land in a more traditional way. Grants are available to maintain hay meadows, heather moors, limestone grassland and the upland landscape in general.

Gibbs Hill is one of the farms involved in the pilot scheme. In exchange for the grant, the farmer has to allow open access to the fell land to the right of the track.

A waymarked Stewardship route providing a circular walk to the north and west rejoins this track at Gibbs Hill. If you wish you may leave the track at the waymarker and follow the alternative route round to Gibbs Hill. Otherwise carry on.

As you walk along it should be easy to identify some landmarks; Walltown Crags lie directly ahead, slightly to the right and nearer are Swallow Crags, and half-left on the horizon, is the distinctive hump of Cold Fell, 621m (2037 feet) in height.

Cross the next two stiles. Go over the bridge, bear right and keep on to the gate. Go through the gate, join the tarmac road, cross the hump-back bridge and begin the long walk uphill.

The rush-covered land to the left is typical of poor hill pasture in this part of the country. Compare this with the land to the right which was improved in the 1970s and 1980s when government grants were given to hill farmers to help increase livestock numbers. The wheel has turned full circle, with farmers now being grant-aided under the Stewardship scheme to let the land revert to a more natural state.

At the top of the hill, cross the cattle grid, turn left and follow the road back to Steel Rigg.

6. Stonehaugh – Linacres – Roses Bower. 8.5km (5½ miles); about 4 hours

A mysterious pool, a highly unusual loo and spectacular views along the Warksburn gorge add to the interest of this long walk. There are a few steep sections but much of the route is across fields and along forest edges with a short stretch on a little-used tarmac road. The ground is generally firm underfoot but can be boggy in places after spells of wet weather.

From Nunwick on the B6320 north-west of Hexham, follow the signs to Stonehaugh 9km (5½ miles) west along an unclassified road. Park at the Forestry Commission picnic site outside the village (GR 789762). Walk up to the road, turn right and pause on the bridge.

The Warksburn, a main tributary of the North Tyne, flows under the bridge. Ahead, over-looking the burn, is the village of Stonehaugh. Like other purpose-built forest villages of the early 1950s it was sited where major plantings were to take place. At first there were open views all round. Gradually the fells were planted up and as the trees grew, so the aspect changed, but it remains an attractive setting.

Continue uphill and at the top of the bank go over the stile by the fingerpost on the left signed Stonehaugh Shields. Follow the direction of the blue waymarkers across the field and through the wicket gates.

Soft rush is quite prolific in this field and whilst it indicates that the land is wet and the grazing poor, it did have its uses in times past. Farmers cut it for winter fodder and for thatching hay-stacks; their wives peeled off the outer green casing to expose the soft white pith which was dried and used like a candle wick to soak up sheep fat from a dish, thus providing a cheap source of light.

Cross the camping field to join a track and follow this round to the front of the farm-house. At the fingerpost follow the path signed to Low Roses Bower through the meadow above the Warksburn.

In spring the banks of the meadow are carpeted in wild flowers. The more obvious are cowslips, primroses and, on the wet flushes, the northern marsh orchid. In summer, betony, germander speedwell and meadowsweet thrive among the old traditional hay grasses, timothy, cocksfoot and wavy hair. It is from this ancient blend of flowers and grasses that the rich scent of newly-mown hay is derived.

Betony

Leave the meadow and follow the line of electricity poles down the forest ride.

Gently finger the laddered needles of the first conifer overhanging the fence, just past the corner post. This is Abies alba, common silver fir. The needles have a distinctive smell of citrus fruits, grapefruit in particular. The arrangement of the needles is unusual; try to identify similar trees as you walk along the forest edge.

Continue on and after a steep dip the route passes into the trees on the left.

As the path threads its way along the edge of the gorge, there are tantalising glimpses of the Warksburn below. Here, the wooded gorge is frequented by sparrowhawks which hunt mainly by surprise. Here the sparrow-hawk catches its prey by dashing through the trees to create panic among the smaller birds. When they take flight, it pounces.

Keep to the path as it bears right into a dense part of the forest.

You are now in a Forest Enterprise plantation which provides timber for the building industry. The trees are Norway spruce which grow tall and straight, giving a high yield of timber per hectare. They are harvested when they are about 40 years old. Notice the absence of undergrowth in the woodland. Lack of light and nutrients means there is very little plant growth here except for fungi which spring up in dark damp places like this in early autumn.

After a short distance turn sharp left by the waymarker, back to the edge of the gorge. Go down the steep, stepped path and leave the woodland by the stile. Continue along the waterside to Holywell Cottage.

Holywell, named after a nearby sulphur well reputed to cure "ague, gravel and other obstructions" was a favourite haunt of F. A. Wills. Writing in the late 1940s/early 1950s under the pseudonym 'Vagabond', he based his guide books and animal stories on his observations in the wild. One of his books 'Still Waters' is set in the Warksburn gorge and includes a reference to the Black Pool by the cottage. It is aptly named 'The Bottomless Linn' for the pool is deep and still with only the occasional ripple from a brown trout to disturb the dark surface.

From the cottage bear right uphill, keeping the line of trees on your left and follow the direction of the waymarker along the ridge.

This hill land is part of the holding of the The Ash Farm and there is open access for walkers through the Countryside Stewardship Scheme set up by the Countryside Commission. Under the scheme which is government funded, landowners in the uplands are encouraged to reduce the number of stock they keep and farm their land in a traditional manner with due regard for nature conservation. In some agreements under Countryside Stewardship, public access off rights of way, has been negotiated. These areas are signed, stiled and waymarked by the farmer/landowner.

Continue on until you reach a ladder stile in the wall ahead.

It is worth pausing to appreciate the extensive views to the east and north. Below, the course of the Warksburn leads your eye eastwards down the Tyne valley as it sweeps left. Turning to the north, you will see the radio mast on Brieredge and then the Hareshaw Fells lying between Tynedale and Redesdale.

At the stile turn left and keeping the fence on your right walk downhill. You are now on the Pennine Way. Follow the signposted route, passing a barn on the left, down a dip then left to the Warksburn.

The isolated hawthorns on the haughland are a good habitat for tree pipits. These small summer visitors are easily identifiable by their unique flight pattern. They rise and fall like a helicopter, singing all the while, before drifting back down to their perch in the hawthorns.

Cross the footbridge and follow the path as it winds steeply up the hillside. Go over the stile and follow the direction of the

Holywell cottage

The Black Pool

waymarker to the right hand corner of the garden wall at Horneystead. From here, take the path indicated by the Pennine Way fingerpost across the fields to The Ash in the trees ahead.

The Ash is a substantial late 18th century Northumbrian farmhouse. Originally only one room deep it was extended at the rear in the mid 19th century. The building was heightened by several courses, re-roofed and the walled garden was added. The conservatory is a 20th century addition designed to fit in with the rest of the house.

Pass in front of the garden, then between a wall on the left and a farm shed on the right. Turn left, make for the field gate, go through the gate, cross the road by Leadgate, over the stile and into the field. The Pennine Way to Lowstead is well defined.

At Lowstead, the main part of the house which has diamond-paned windows, together with the adjoining building on the left, date from the 16th century. Both are bastle houses. Their thick walls provided some security for the occupants from the attacks by the Border Reivers. The stone staircase was added in the 18th century when the reivers had ceased to trouble the folk of North Tynedale. The garden

in front of the house was once a farmyard, with byres, stables, a cart shed and a granary grouped round about.

Keep to the path as it goes through the garden at Lowstead, taking care to close any gates. Go out along the access road which bends to the right and cross a cattle grid. At the next junction, leave the Pennine Way and turn sharp left downhill and pause on the bridge over the Blacka Burn.

Notice the geological strata in the bottom of the burn, massive blocks of stone laid down like a pavement 300 million years ago, when layers of carboniferous rocks were being formed in the shallow sea which covered this area at that time.

Walk uphill to Linacres and keeping the farmhouse on the left, go through the yard then bear right along a track beside a walled copse on the left. From the corner of the wall go straight ahead and make for the gate at the far side of the field. Go through the gate and head across to the corner of the conifer plantation. Turn left along the edge of the woodland. After about 1km, recross the Blacka Burn by the footbridge.

The planting scheme on the right is part of a forestry conservation project. Hardwood species have been planted near the burn to provide a wildlife corridor and along the edge of the conifers to break up the regimented blocks.

Continue uphill. Cross a stile by the gate, past the sheep pens on the right and keep on to join the tarmac road. Go straight ahead on the road until you reach a fingerpost signed Low Roses Bower on the left. Cross the stile and keeping the fence on the right make for Low Roses Bower.

These derelict buildings were once the home of the head of the Milburns, one of the main North Tyne families renowned for their reiving activities. The group includes the remains of a 17th century bastle with late 18th century additions and an incredible outside netty

(toilet), known as the Long Drop. The derivation is obvious for this earth closet is suspended fully 12m (40 feet) above the Warksburn gorge with only a basic toilet seat between the user and certain death on the rocks below! Occupied until relatively recently, Low Roses Bower used to be a popular meeting place for local barn dances. Imagine coming out to use the netty on a cold, dark, windy night; it must have taken considerable courage.

Keeping the buildings on your right, follow the path round in the direction of the finger-post signed Holywell and walk downhill to the burn. Cross over the footbridge, turn right and retrace the outward route back to Stonehaugh.

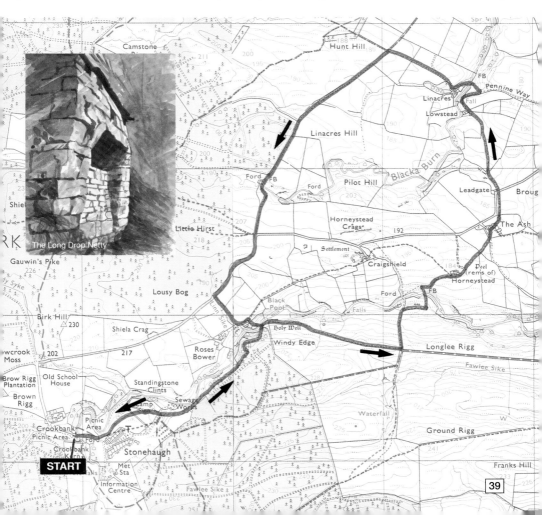

The Long Drop Netty

7

Hareshaw Linn.
5km (3 miles); about 2 hours

An easy walk following the Hareshaw Burn up through a steep-sided wooded valley to an impressive waterfall, the Linn, and back. This is not a walk to be hurried; there is much to see and appreciate. The path can be wet and muddy in places, even during dry weather, so stout footwear is recommended.

From the main street in Bellingham take the road signposted West Woodburn. Go over the bridge, take the first turn left and park in the National Park car park (GR 841835).

The Hareshaw Burn drains an area of high ground to the north of Bellingham and flows into the North Tyne just south of the town itself. The picturesque dene has always been a popular walk for local people. In the late 19th century the townsfolk laid a cobbled path and built six bridges over the burn to improve access to the Linn and to their favourite picnic place nearby. The whole of Hareshaw Dene and its waterfall are now owned and managed by Northumberland National Park.

Turn right out of the car park, go past Foundry Farm, through the kissing gate and follow the path round to the right of the hill.

The hill is actually waste material from the old Hareshaw Ironworks which operated here in the 1840s. Iron from this foundry was used to build Newcastle's High Level Bridge, opened in 1849. As there was no railway link with Bellingham at the time, the costs of transportation by road were high. The Company was unable to compete with other firms who had the advantage of a rail outlet and was forced to close after eight years of production. The only buildings that have survived from the once extensive works are the offices which have been converted to the terrace of stone cottages at Foundry Farm. The derelict site of the former Ironworks, now a Scheduled Ancient Monument, was acquired by Northumberland County Council in 1979 and

given to the National Park to manage.

Continue on, through another kissing gate and into the grassland.

Due to the nature of the spoil heaps the soil in this area of grassland is richer in lime than that in neighbouring fields, so the flora is more varied. Butterflies are particularly in evidence in June, when the meadow brown, small heath, common blue and green-veined white are on the wing.

Meadow brown butterfly

The grassland is managed by allowing cattle and sheep to graze the area from autumn to spring. This helps prevent the expansion of scrub, particularly hawthorn and creeping willow which allows a rich variety of summer flowers to flourish.

Follow the path and enter the wood through the wicket gate.

The importance of this woodland for its great diversity of plant and wildlife, in particular the lichen communities on the wych elm trees, has been recognised by English Nature (formerly the Nature Conservancy Council) and the area is now a Site of Special Scientific Interest (SSSI).

The National Park Authority bought the wood in 1974 to protect it and safeguard it for informal recreation. It had been put on the market after the County Council had refused the owner permission to fell some of the more mature trees.

Until the 1980s most of the trees in the lower part of the wood were wych elm but with the spread of Dutch elm disease the composition of the wood is changing. As the elm slowly disappears, ash, which dominates the upper reaches, is beginning to establish itself. Young saplings are already growing quickly on either side of the path.

Continue on the path until you reach the wayside seat.

Most of this wood is classed as ancient semi-natural, which means there has been tree cover here for at least 500 years and probably as far back as the end of the last Ice Age, about 10,000 years ago. It is semi-natural in that throughout the last five centuries it has been managed in some way, possibly by coppicing, by local folk.

By contrast there are two examples of plantation woodland close by, Scots pine on the left, oak on the right. Because they are native species, they too are of great value to the wildlife community. The oak woodland in particular, provides homes for many resident birds and for summer visitors such as wood warbler, pied flycatcher and redstart.

Follow the path downhill to cross the first of the six footbridges.

To the left of the path are several dead logs which like all decomposing matter actually support many different life forms. Wood lice, millipedes, slugs and spiders like the dark, damp conditions on the woodland floor. If you stand quietly you can sometimes hear rustling sounds made by blackbirds picking over the leaf litter in search of a juicy morsel.

Fungi found throughout the woodland in autumn, also live off dead logs and fallen trees. One of the most deadly, as far as trees are concerned is the honey fungus. It's often known as 'bootlace' fungus because of its long rhizoids (root hairs) which travel underneath the bark and through the soil, carrying wet rot disease infecting and eventually killing live trees. It has been described as the greatest natural threat to British forestry because there is still no effective control for the disease.

Honey fungus

Continue on the woodland path as it crosses and recrosses the burn, counting the bridges as you go.

Lesser celandine

Ramsons (wild garlic)

Primrose

Apart from the trees, the woodland has its own particular flora. In spring, before the leaves begin to blot out the light, the banksides are carpeted in yellow and white flowers; lesser celandine, primrose, the delicate wood sorrel and the pungent wild garlic. Other woodland flowers appear in summer, stitchwort, red campion, water avens, foxglove and meadow sweet. There are wild raspberries too, and in autumn an abundance of acorns and hazel nuts. This plentiful supply of food supports a high population of insects, birds and other woodland creatures such as red squirrel, wood mouse and bank vole.

In autumn, squirrels bury their food in shallow holes in the ground. When winter comes and they wake to feed, they don't always remember where they have hidden all

Common polypody fern

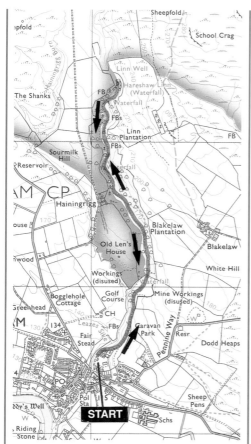

Thuidium tameriscinum. The fern on the top of the boulders is common polypody which is also growing on the branches of many of the trees nearby. This fern is usually found in deep, shaded valleys like Hareshaw, where the humidity is higher. Not surprisingly, Hareshaw with its own micro-climate is one of the best places in the county for mosses and ferns; over 300 species have been identified.

Cross the last footbridge and head for the Linn.

The path ends abruptly with dramatic views of the Linn and its plunge pool. The water pours over the bedrock with tremendous force even in summer when there is less rainwater draining off the hills. The water cascading over the edge of the fall is gradually wearing away the bands of softer rocks, shales, and as it does so, it undercuts the overlying layer of harder rock, sandstone, which then collapses into the burn. In this way the waterfall is slowly moving upstream and in time the valley will become even deeper.

The cliffs at the top of the Linn are inhabited by jackdaws, a bird that often nests around buildings, particularly in chimney pots. In spring and early summer they can be heard calling to one another with a distinctive 'Jack,Jack' from which they get their name Jackdaw. Their food consists mainly of grassland pests such as leather jackets which they find on the fields and rough grazing above the waterfall.

Jackdaw

the nuts and seeds. Some of these survive and put down roots. In this way squirrels help to spread the natural woods.

After the fifth bridge, pause again.

The large conifer to the right of the path is a Douglas fir. This is an imported species; it originates on the north-west seaboard of North America and was first discovered by Archibald Menzies, a great plant collector. It was brought to this country by Sir David Douglas from whom it gets its common name; Menzies is commemorated in its latin name Pseudotsuga menziesii.

Continue on, over the wooden walkway until you reach some large boulders on the right.

The boulders are covered with several species of mosses and ferns, including one of the most beautiful of the common woodland mosses,

8

Bellingham – The Riding Wood – The North Tyne.
5km (3 miles);
about 2½ hours

The market town of Bellingham is the starting point for this walk which takes in high moorland, a lovely oak wood, a Romano-British settlement and part of the old Border Counties Railway.
It finishes with an easy return along the scenic banks of the River North Tyne. The outward route involves a climb up gentle gradients; there are no difficult sections and whilst conditions underfoot can be muddy in places the going is generally firm.

Park in Bellingham. The walk begins at the Tourist Information Centre/Fountain Cottage Tearooms at the north end of the main street (GR 839836).

For most of the year Bellingham (pronounced Bellin-jam) is a peaceful little market town. Its shops and businesses serve smaller communities and isolated farms throughout the North Tyne and Upper Rede valleys. But in summer, the pace of life quickens when many Pennine Way backpackers and visitors arrive in the area. However, the annual autumn sales of sheep and cattle are the main event of the year. Shepherds, stock and wagons overwhelm Bellingham and major traffic congestion is not unknown!

Bellingham's long history as a border town at the mercy of warring armies and rapacious reivers is reflected in the narrowness of its oldest streets and in its fortified church. Try to find time to explore.

From the TIC, walk back along the main street and turn right up the lane beside Barclay's Bank. Near the top of the lane pause to look across to the pens on your right.

This is Bellingham Mart. More than 50,000 sheep and 1500 cattle pass through these pens every year. There has been a mart here for more than 100 years but sales are only held from late August to November, with another in January and one in May. Each autumn there are special sales for hill lambs, spring-born calves, beef cattle and beef breeding stock.

In the old days before there were wagons to transport animals to the mart, only shepherds out of the North Tyne and Rede Valleys went to Bellingham because there was a limit to the distance their animals could be driven on foot. Wagons have made a huge difference. Today sellers come from all over Northumberland, from Cumbria and from Scotland; buyers come from as far afield as the south of England and Wales.

Bellingham Mart

Continue on. Bear right past the bungalows on the right, then turn right along a street of bungalows. Follow the road round into the cul-de-sac. At the end, turn right onto a footpath and follow this along the side of the houses, down into the dip, up and over the stile and into the field. With the fence on your right go uphill, through the wicket gate and turn left along the tarmac road.

This section affords ample opportunity to enjoy distant views over the North Tyne Valley. The wooded landscape is a picture at all times of the year but is at its best when the warm colours of autumn bring a richer quality to the scene. Ash trees are the first to change colour, from green to lemon yellow, then sycamore, beech – a lovely burnt orange – and finally oak which usually holds its leaves into November.

At the Reenes Farm, follow the waymarked route between the farm buildings, then pause on the open road to look left across the valley.

The large mansion in the trees is Hesleyside Hall, seat of the Charltons. The best-known story about this family is that of the Charlton spur. In reiving days when their store of meat was exhausted, a spur on a platter was brought to the table as a sign that it was time for the menfolk to ride out on another raid to restock the larder!

Records show there was a tower at Hesleyside in 1525 when the 50 strong garrison was attacked by Scottish Reivers. After peace was restored to the Borders in the late 17th century a more comfortable house was built onto the tower. Then came two disastrous fires which resulted in various alterations and extensions and sadly, the tower was pulled down. Apart from the beautiful Georgian mansion, Hesleyside is noted for its magnificent woods, parkland and avenues of trees; the whole estate is a good example of sensitive landscape design.

Continue to West Reenes. Keep straight ahead, cross the stile in the fence, then bear slightly left across the field and go over another stile in the fence opposite. Carry on in the same direction across uneven ground towards the drystone wall ahead.

The unevenness of the ground was caused by quarrying into the rock which outcrops along the whole of this ridge.

The stone was used to build local roads.

The next waymarker is alongside the grass-covered remains of a round house in a Romano-British farming settlement, part of which has been destroyed by quarrying.

Continue on to join the track running alongside the wall. Keeping the wall on your left, carry on uphill and cross the stile by the field gate. Keep on past the lone pine on the left and follow the waymarked route to the end of the ridge.

Make your way gradually downhill past two stone cairns, cross the burn and follow it to the bottom of the hill. Recross the burn, turn right and go through the gate in the field wall straight ahead. Bear left to the corner of the wall and follow the way-markers into The Riding Wood.

Natural oak woodland is a rare feature in today's upland landscape. The Riding Wood is not fenced off and excessive grazing by sheep and cattle has meant that even in years when there has been a good crop of acorns the resulting young trees have not survived. To ensure that the wood has a future, any seedlings which appear naturally are now protected by plastic tubes provided by the National Park. Oak woodland is a haven for many song birds, in particular redstart, wood warbler and pied flycatcher.

The oak wood is also the site of a Romano-British farming settlement occupied about 1800 years ago. It was excavated in 1958. The site is enclosed by a low stone wall, surrounded by a ditch and earth bank. On the higher, drier land towards the back of the settlement are traces of three round houses. At the front (east end), are two stock-proof cattle yards, one on either side of the raised, central pathway. These yards appear as shallow, boggy depressions where rushes now grow.

Romano-British settlement in Riding Wood

Follow the waymarkers through the wood. Go downhill and cross the wooden footbridge over the old Border Counties railway line.

Had you crossed this bridge before 1958 you may well have seen a steam train passing by. The green track below is the most obvious reminder that the Border Counties Railway came this way. In the early 1850s investors from the south of England and 159 local people from all walks of life financed the Border Counties Railway Company. William Henry Charlton of Hesleyside was elected Company Chairman. The line from Hexham to Riccarton on the other side of the Border was finally completed in 1862; 98 years later the rails were lifted and another important part of the local way of life passed into history.

The footbridge has been renovated by the National Park Voluntary Warden Service who painted it and laid new decking.

Continue down to the fence. Cross the stile, turn left along the road. Forest vehicles often use this road so take care to keep into the verge and face the oncoming traffic.

Go past a layby and at the next bend cross the waymarked stile and follow the well-worn path along the riverside.

Following the clean-up of its lower reaches in the 1980s, the Tyne has been claimed as one of the best salmon-fishing rivers in the country. Here on the North Tyne, you may see salmon leaping as they make their way up the river in autumn on their spawning run. But for the greater part of the year you are more likely to see rings of ripples on the placid water where trout and young salmon have risen to take flies from the surface.

The smaller fish attract fish-eating birds such as goosander and cormorant. Both are seen regularly on the river, cormorant as far upstream as Kielder Water. Collectively these birds take a large percentage of fish stocks and because of this they are unpopular with anglers.

Another water bird to look out for along the river, is the mallard. The nest is often several hundred yards from the water, but as soon as they are hatched, the downy young are led to the safety of the river. The male plays no part in incubation or in raising the family. With such bright colours he would be a give-away to any predator.

Continue following the river downstream until you reach a kissing gate. Go through the gate, keep on under the arched bridge and carry on to the end of the riverside path. Go up the steps in the river defence and turn right. Follow the path as it bears round to the left past a car repair workshop on the right and St. Cuthbert's Well on the left. Turn left into Brookside Place, through the square and back to your car.

River North Tyne, near Bellingham

Track bed of the Border Counties Railway, near Riding Wood ❯

A Class J21 special waiting at Bellingham station on Show Day, about 1950

9 Chirdonburn Bridge – Whitchester – Cadger Ford – Dally Castle. 7km (4½ miles); about 3 hours

The Chirdon Burn is one of the less well-known valleys in the Upper North Tyne. Much of the land is given over to sheep farming but a number of wild creatures also make their home here.

After a gentle ascent from the meadow, the path continues upwards, skirting the edge of Snabdaugh (pronounced Snabduff) Moor to Whitchester Farm. A rough track leads downhill to the bridge at Cadger Ford. The remainder of the walk on a little-used tarmac road follows the north bank of the Chirdon Burn and makes a short diversion to the ruins of Dally Castle before returning to the start.

From Bellingham take the C200 (Kielder Water). After 6km (3½ miles) cross Tarset Bridge, turn left signed Hesleyside and after 1km park in the layby at Chirdonburn Bridge (GR 783850).

Sir John Swinburne, one of the great North Tyne landowners paid for Chirdonburn Bridge to be built in 1821, to replace the ford which was dangerous when the burn was in flood. The source of the burn lies 19km (12 miles) west of here on the bleak and desolate slopes of Humble Hill and Black Knowe. The large catchment area consists mainly of blanket peat which holds the water like a sponge but once the peat becomes saturated, water runs off very quickly causing the burn to rise rapidly. For this reason Chirdonburn Bridge has a high arch, a feature common to other 19th century stone-built bridges in the North Tyne Valley.

Set off along the road in the direction of Snabdaugh Farm. At the fingerpost signed Whitchester turn right onto a grassy track. Go through the gate and follow the path across the field to the fence by the burn.

One of the pleasures of this part of the walk is the sound of the burn running along its stony bed. In earlier times waterworn cobbles were used to surface roads, paths and farmyards.

Keeping the fence on your right continue on to reach the field wall. Turn left to walk alongside the wall and, passing a field gate on your right, go through the gate in the fence ahead. Turn immediately right and go through another gate in the wall. Follow the grassy bank straight ahead. Continue uphill on the bank for about 91m (100 yards). Pause to look back down the valley.

In the middle distance on the hillside, halfway between the hamlet of Lanehead and the River North Tyne, is a large mound. This is the site of Tarset Castle. It was here in 1524 that Hector Charlton of the Bower gave Easter Communion (Mass) to the local reivers. He had stolen wine and 800 wafers from St. Cuthbert's Church Bellingham. The service was in defiance of Cardinal Thomas Wolsey's decree closing all the churches in Tynedale because both clergy and parishioners were "wicked"!

Tormentil

Carry on, keeping to the bank which borders the edge of Snabdaugh Moor until you reach a tumbled wall across the path.

From late spring this grassy bank cropped by sheep and rabbits, is speckled with yellow tormentil. In medieval days, the roots and flowers of this dainty plant were reputed to cure a variety of ills ranging from toothache to diarrhoea – hence the name torment-il!

Left of the bank and running parallel, is a broad, slightly raised track. Within living memory this used to be the road from Whitchester to Snabdaugh and on down to

Kestrel

crows. Occasionally around the base you can find kestrel pellets – regurgitated indigestible remains of their last meal. If you look closely at one of them you will notice it is made up of mouse fur and beetle wing-cases. Unlike owls, kestrels can digest bone and do not swallow their food whole.

When your reach the top, pause to appreciate the view all round.

To the right (north-west), across the great expanse of Kielder Forest and rising out of the trees, is Deadwater Fell; at its feet is the infant North Tyne. North-east lies Hareshaw Common, the high moorland fell separating the North Tyne and Rede Valleys; to the south-east, Shitlington Common while to the south-west is the sombre outline of Wark Forest.

Bellingham. In the late 18th and early 19th centuries when small-scale coal workings were operating near Hart Crags, sturdy packhorses plodded down this track with heavy panniers of coal strapped to their sides.

Cross the wall, bear left and make for the first of a series of waymarkers which indicate the route to the top of the fell.

These waymarkers are often used as perches or look-out posts by kestrels and carrion

Bear left to avoid boggy ground and carry on to Whitchester Farm.

Although the farm dates to the early 19th century, the main period of land improvement in the uplands, the actual name is much older. In 1604 James I's Border Commissioners reported that a survey made in the reign of the King's great, great grandfather Henry VII,

View across the North Tyne Valley towards Leonard's Hill

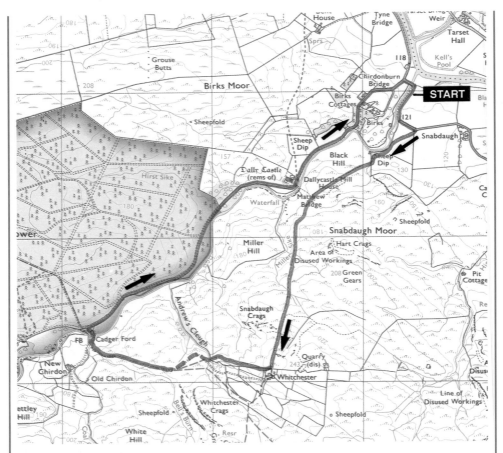

mentioned Whitchester as just one of several tenements (the others being Roughside, Snabdaugh and Chirdon), held by the Heron family who lived at Chipchase Castle near Wark.

In those days Whitchester land would have been used only for summer grazing; today it is a working hill farm. At 220m (600 feet) above sea level, it occupies an exposed position. The small conifer plantation provides shelter for the farm buildings from the prevailing west wind.

Turn right in front of the farm gate and, keeping the plantation on your left, walk downhill to cross a small burn and join the farm track.

This is part of the route of the Border County Ride, a long distance bridleway developed and promoted by Northumberland National Park in partnership with The British Horse Society, Forest Enterprise and the Ministry of Defence.

Continue down the track until you reach the Chirdon Burn. Pause on the bridge.

Mayfly

On still summer days large numbers of mayflies dance above the water. Mayfly is really a misnomer because they can be seen throughout the summer months. The eggs are laid in the water and for at least a year the resulting 'nymphs' live a precarious life clinging to the leeward side of submerged rocks and stone. The nymph stage is followed by the 'dun' or pre-adult stage which lasts a few hours and turns the mayfly from a water creature to a winged insect. The adult stage lasts another few hours long enough to find a mate, lay eggs and fall exhausted and dying into the water.

Mayflies are an important source of food for swallows, wagtails and dippers and also for fish. Not surprisingly, anglers have designed artificial flies similar in appearance to the mayfly as a tempting lure.

Leave the bridge and follow the track round to the road. Turn right. Continue along the valley passing the conifer plantation and then an old alder wood on the left.

On the way you may notice beech, horse chestnut and Leyland cypress growing along the roadside verges. These trees were planted purely for their ornamental value by the forester who lived at the Bower, in the early days of the Forestry Commission's work in the Chirdonburn. He wanted to make his daily drive down this road more interesting and attractive. Other private planting schemes can be found along burns elsewhere in the Kielder Forests.

As the road emerges from the trees the site of Dally Castle is visible just ahead. After rounding the bend in the road cross the stile on the left and walk up the hillside to the ruins.

Dipper

Not much remains of this small medieval castle but it is easy to see why it was built here. It sits on a glacial ridge, a natural defensive position overlooking the Chirdon Burn. A ditch dug across the promontory to the west of the castle made the site even more secure. The sturdy walls are buttressed on the north side; blocked-up loopholes are visible in places.

A Scot, Sir David Lindsay, built Dally in 1257 but its fortifications were never finished. It probably continued to be used as a stronghold until the reign of James I (1603-1625) and then it gradually fell into ruin. During the 19th century the stone pillars supporting the upper floor were used for a piggery and most of the remaining masonry went into building the corn mill and the Mill House by the burn.

Retrace your steps to the road. Continue on through more open countryside. Go past Birks Cottages, cross Chirdonburn Bridge and return to your parking place.

The ruins of Dally Castle

10

Slaty Ford – Donkleywood.
6.5km (4 miles);
about 2½ hours

A scenic walk along an old drove road with views over open countryside, followed by a gentle descent to the wooded banks of the North Tyne. Some of the loveliest hay meadows in the National Park line the banks.

From Bellingham take the C200 (Kielder Water). After 13km (8 miles) turn right into Falstone. Go under the railway bridge and turn right to reach the start of the walk in 2km (1¼ miles). Park on the grass verge under the Scots pines near the junction with the unclassified road signed 'unsuitable for motor vehicles after 1 mile' (GR 741866). Walk up the unclassified road to the bend.

The roughly-dressed stone post standing on the left is a reminder that there used to be a gate across the road here. It was hung on iron crooks, one of which is still firmly in place. The crooks were fixed in with molten lead, a difficult job which required a steady hand. First the post was drilled and the crook inserted, then the hole was surrounded with a funnel of clay and the hot lead carefully ladled in. The clay was removed when the lead had set.

Continue on along the road.

Over the stone wall to the left, the hillside is covered with clumps of soft rush. This smooth-stemmed plant thrives on badly-drained ground and has no feeding value for stock.

Go through the gate ahead.

On the right, and parallel to the road, are the remains of a field wall. The stone has been taken away to rebuild other walls in the area. Drystone walls are a traditional feature of the upland landscape. They are a testament to the large number of people who once lived and worked in the countryside. Most walls date from the late 18th century when the land was enclosed before improvement was carried out.

Keep on, through the next gate.

The road crosses the Donkleywood Burn. Hawthorn trees grow on the banksides, self-planted from seeds carried by birds; they make excellent nesting sites for mistle thrushes, finches and sometimes carrion crows.

Go past the entrance to Ryeclose Farm. Follow the rutted track and go through another gate.

To the left is the southern edge of Falstone Forest, one of several plantations which together make up the huge forest of Kielder.

Straight ahead, on the distant hillside, the dark line of the track winds its way to Lanehead where it becomes a tarmac road again and continues on to Bellingham. In the old days, this was the route followed by the North Tyne herds who drove their flocks down the valley to the annual sales at the Mart.

Continue past some old sheep pens on the left and go through the next gate onto the open moor.

This was once a glorious heather moor but most of the heather has died out as a result of overgrazing by cattle. Molinia grass has largely replaced the heather.

Stay on the track. Go through another gate and stop at Slaty Ford.

The sandstone bed of the Thorney Burn forms a natural ford. It's a pleasant place to stop. The shallow, slow-flowing water is a perfect habitat for dragonflies. Hawker dragonflies often hold territories here; the females laying their eggs in quieter stretches of water.

Hawker dragonfly

Mosses and liverworts cling to the crevices in the rocks, thriving in the cool, damp conditions. Downy or hairy birch grows by the waterfall and in the wet flushes on the steep bankside, there is dwarf willow and butterwort, one of Britain's few insectivorous plants.

Retrace your steps back through the gate. Turn left along the side of the wall. Go over the stile, turn right and follow the waymarked route across the moor.

This type of moorland is ideal for ground-nesting birds such as skylark. Their nests, concealed in a tuft of grass, are very difficult to find. The eggs are dark and speckled, the colour of the matted grass which forms the nest. If a sitting bird is disturbed, it never flies straight up but scuttles away through the grass like a mouse, before taking flight.

Continue on keeping the burn on your left, until you reach a wicket gate. Go through this gate and the next two in the fences ahead. Pass in front of Hill House and go through the next wicket into the field. Walk diagonally across the field passing to the left of two trees.

To the right is a National Park tree planting scheme. About 500 saplings – oak, ash, hazel, alder – are now well-established. Tubes protect the young trees from the ravages of weather and rabbits. The tubes are bio-degradable and will eventually break up and rot. At the bottom of the slope a pond, grant-aided by the National Park, has been created

to provide an interesting wildlife habitat.

Walk towards the two stone gate posts. Go through the gate, cross the old railway line, go through the gate ahead and into the field. Leave by the wicket gate and turn right onto the road, past Old Hall Cottage. Follow the road until you reach a fingerpost on the left signed Donkleywood.

Hay meadow

The field you are passing on the left just beyond Old Hall is a traditional hay meadow

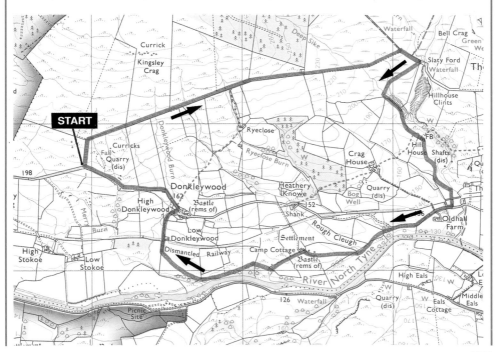

with a rich variety of colourful flowers and fine grasses in season. The hay is cut after the seeds have set. Neither artificial fertilisers nor pesticides are used, just farmyard manure (not slurry!). Hay meadows are not only visually attractive but they represent a traditional type of land management that has largely disappeared as a result of incentives to increase agricultural production in the post-war period.

Since the Second World War Britain has lost 95% of its traditional hay meadows. This is one of a few which survive in the National Park. It is at its best in June and July when sorrel, yellow rattle, bush vetch and ox-eye daisies are in flower.

At the signpost descend the steep grassy bank to the Ryeclose Burn. Cross the footbridge and go straight uphill to the fence. Cross the step stile and follow the direction of the waymarker across another hay field. Please keep to the path before going over the stile beside the old oak tree.

Keeping the fence on your right walk downhill and around to a metal fieldgate. Cross the stile and walk in the direction of the waymarker uphill to Camp Cottage.

A small heap of rubble at the south-east corner of the farm buildings is all that remains of a bastle house that once stood here.

After crossing the next stile keep the wooden fence on your right and walk around the front of Camp Cottage to another stile. Go over this and walk down the edge of the field, crossing two more stiles. Turn right and follow the path around the hillside until you reach yet another stile into a wood. Continue on the woodland path.

This is a lovely stretch of riverside woodland. Most of the trees are oak, probably planted

100 years ago; there are some alder and the outer fringe is all self-planted birch. In late spring the woodland is alive with songbirds. It is a favourite hunting ground for the sparrowhawk which lays its eggs early so the young can benefit from the glut of prey.

Leave the wood when you come to a stone wall in the field on your right. Go through the gap in the wall and follow the direction of the waymarker diagonally across the field and up to the track leading onto the bridge over the old railway.

From the bridge there is a good view down to the track bed of the former Border Counties Railway. The railway arrived in 1860 long before a good road existed and for many years it was the lifeline of the valley.

Walk down into Donkleywood. The track bears right, through the little hamlet.

Donkleywood is one of the oldest documented settlements in North Tynedale. As early as 1166 Duncliueshalch was recorded as the site of one of the hunting lodges of William the Lion of Scotland, who held the Liberty of Tynedale from the English Kings. By 1279 Donkleywood had become one of the seven main townships in the area.

Turn left past the small triangular village green and follow the road uphill, back to your car.

North Tyne Valley near Donkleywood

Diamond Cottage – Ridley Shiel – Black Middens – Gatehouse. 9.5km (6 miles); about 2½ - 3 hours

In the 16th century when trouble was rife throughout the Border country, the Tarset Valley was often raided by bands of reivers. In September 1584 for instance, 300 Scottish Reivers led by 'Kinmont Willie' Armstrong carried out a daring raid during daylight hours. They stole 140 cattle, 60 horses and 500 sheep; set fire to 60 houses and killed 10 men. This walk takes you past three bastles which survived this devastating attack.

The route follows a disused road over high moorland, to cross the Black Burn and returns by way of the forest and the Tarset Valley. The going is easy and apart from a gentle walk uphill on grass to Black Middens bastle and back, conditions underfoot are good.

From Greenhaugh, follow the signs to Black Middens bastle as far as the minor crossroads (GR 792892). Park past the side entrance of Diamond Cottage, on the grass verge of the disused road signed No Through Road. Walk up the road and through the gate.

Drystone walls such as the one on the left are a feature of the landscape in this area. Many of these walls are a hundred years old or more and are now in need of repair. This is some-thing the National Park can help farmers with. Grants of up to 60% are available to offset what would otherwise be a very expensive project.

In open country where there is little natural cover, drystone walls provide nesting sites for birds such as pied wagtail and wheatear. Wheatears are migrants, spending the winter in Africa and arriving back in Britain in March or April. The eggs are laid deep in a hole in walls or in rock outcrops where their young will be safe from predators.

Go on until you reach Belling Rigg lime kiln on the right.

The kiln, like the drystone walls in the area, is built of locally quarried sandstone. It has three 'eyes' with corbelled arches and there is a blocked-up flue at the base of the central eye. The limestone was quarried from outcrops nearby. There is evidence of quarrying right along the shoulder of the hill, but no trace of bell pits in the area, so it is probable that coal to fire the kilns was carted from the Pit Houses colliery in the Tarret Burn, a tributary of the Tarset Burn.

The Belling Rigg kiln dates from the late 18th century and is one of four lime kilns in the National Park singled out for conservation because of their historical interest and the contribution they have made to the character of the landscape. The kilns are a reminder of the great changes that took place in farming practice two hundred years ago. The burnt lime they produced was used to reduce the natural acidity of the upland soils and improve the quality of the grass. Good grazing was needed to feed the increasing number of sheep and cattle required to supply Britain`s rapidly expanding industrial population.

Continue on through the next gate.

In summer, adders sometimes slumber on the track. Tightly coiled they can easily be mistaken for a cow pat! Adders are Britain`s only poisonous snake and as a rule pose no threat, but if aggravated they will strike in self defence. So if you do see one, observe it quietly from a safe distance but don't touch!

Adder

Adders have a dark zig-zag pattern down the middle of their back. Males are smaller and more brightly coloured than the females. They can be grey or greenish with black markings; the females are various shades of brown with dark brown markings. Adders are active during the day and night, feeding on small mammals such as mice, voles and lizards.

Follow the road along the hillside to the bend.

The view ahead and left is virtually all forest with few exceptions. To the north-west, in the far distance and beyond the confines of the trees, rises the bleak fell of Emblehope Moor, where dwarf birch, a relict plant of post-glacial times still survives. Ridley Shiel is in the middle distance and to the right, the broad open expanse of Blackburn Common which forms part of the long ridge between North Tynedale and Redesdale. It is a wild, empty landscape and it is an uphill struggle trying to make a living in such difficult country.

Continue on as the road gradually descends to the burn.

The sheep in this area are Swaledales or Swaledale crosses. They do better on rough, wet grassland than other breeds. Many hill farmers prefer them to the Scottish blackface because they are hardier and survive well in such exposed conditions. Pure-bred Swales are smaller than the blackface. They have straight forelegs, a grey muzzle and grey 'spectacles' and a longer, more pearly fleece. They are easily crossed with other breeds, especially the blue-faced Leicester, to produce breeding ewes called mules. They also make excellent mothers and generally have few problems in lambing.

Swaledale sheep

Pause by the bridge across the Black Burn.

In spring and summer small ungrazed places such as this beside the burn are starred with wild flowers, a reminder of what the higher moorlands must have looked like before the forest blanketed the landscape. Here in early spring you can see the purple wild violet; the yellow tormentil which flowers throughout the summer and in August and September there's the bright blue of the devil's-bit scabious.

Cross the bridge, turn left onto the forest road and after a short distance, left again. Follow the road through the forest for about a mile.

The systematic planting of open moorland has meant a loss of habitat for many plants and in particular, for ground-nesting birds such as snipe, red grouse and partridge, along with the curlew, emblem of Northumberland National Park. But for numerous other species conifer forests have proved beneficial.

Curlew

Newly planted areas are quickly colonised by meadow pipits, whinchats and whitethroats, which favour open country where plants aren't cropped by grazing sheep. As the conifers grow, woodland species such as blackbird, song thrush, willow warbler and robin move in. Eventually the herbs and grasses are shaded out. Yet the tops of these forest giants provide a haven for other birds which need the canopy for feeding and nesting. Amongst them is Europe's smallest bird, the goldcrest with its distinctive twittering call, and the sparrowhawk, one of our most widespread birds of prey. When the trees are felled, the cycle starts all over again.

Pass the barrier near the end of the forest

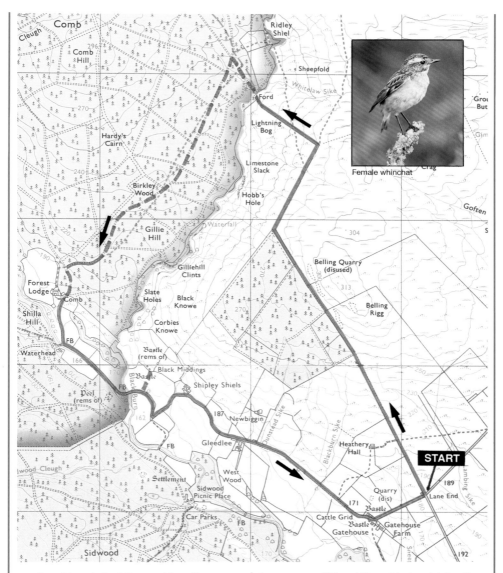

Female whinchat

**road and turn left at the next junction.
Continue on past the Comb on your right.**

The Comb was once a small outbye farm. Now it is an outdoor action centre which offers everything from organised strategy games to team building and leadership courses. Evidence of some of the activities can be seen as you continue on the next stage of the walk beside the Tarset Burn. The burn rises in the peat bogs of Emblehope Moor and drains large areas of Tarset Forest before joining the North Tyne at Tarset Hall.

The woodland along the banks of the burn includes hazel, alder, birch and bird cherry. All these species are native to the British Isles. The bird cherry is most distinctive in spring with its spikes of creamy-white fragrant flowers which blossom in late May. The fruits which ripen in July and August are small, black and very bitter.

Gatehouse Bastle *(with kind permission of the owner)*

Continue on until you reach Black Middens car park on the left. Leave the road, pass through the kissing gate and walk uphill to visit Black Middens bastle.

The Tarset Valley is bastle country. More of these small defensible farmhouses were built here than anywhere else in the National Park as this valley was one of the favourite targets of reivers from Liddesdale. It was virtually impossible to catch the raiders because they were well-mounted on their hardy fell ponies, 'bog-trotters', and were familiar with the lie of the land.

Retrace your steps to the car park, turn left and follow the road round to Shipley Shiels.

In summer the roadside verges are alive with flowers, bees and butterflies.

As the road climbs steeply up to Shipley Shiels, notice the large beech tree on the left. It must be about 150 years old and would have been planted by man because beech is not native to this part of the world. Fine grained and knot free, beech was grown for its timber value, especially in the making of furniture such as round- backed chairs which used to feature in most farmhouse kitchens.

Continue on to Gatehouse.

This tiny hamlet has two bastles. The one on

the left as you reach Gatehouse, is probably one of the most impressive in the county. Apart from the roof of Welsh slate, this bastle, which is privately owned, has scarcely been changed since it was built in the late 16th century. Massive rough-hewn trunks of oak and ash support the upper floor, where the original stone fireplace is still in place.

The bastle on the right had fallen into disrepair but has recently been re-roofed and is now used for storage.

Follow the road round to Diamond Cottage.

In August, the ditch to the left of the road is full of purple-flowering marsh woundwort. It is a very hairy plant and was used successfully in the past to staunch bleeding wounds because the hairs helped the blood to coagulate.

If crushed however the whole plant gives off a stinking smell.

Pause briefly as you pass the front of Diamond Cottage before rounding the corner to your car.

The name is intriguing but a glance at the roof will reveal all! When the cottage was built in 1831 it was probably single storey. The ground floor is stone built and the first floor is of brick which suggests that it was added at a later date.

Falstone – Hawkhope Hill.
3.5km (2 miles);
about 1½ hours

Set against a backdrop of forest and fell and overlooking the River North Tyne, Falstone is an attractive starting point for this short walk.

After leaving the village, the route crosses rough hill land which can be soft underfoot. The next stretch is through woodland. Coming out of the trees, you join a forest track and thereafter the going is firm.

The walk affords a magnificent view over Kielder Water and the potential for seeing some of the forest wildlife.

Park outside the village hall at the west end of Falstone (GR 723876). Walk through the village past the United Reformed Church on the left.

This was a Presbyterian Church until the Presbyterians and Methodists united in 1970. From the late 17th century, Falstone was one of the strongholds of Scottish Presbyterianism in Northumberland. Church records show that ministers and elders kept a watchful eye on the spiritual welfare and morals of their flock. They remonstrated against everything from "want of punctuality in attending funerals, trampling on the grass outside the Meeting House and the growing evil of drink". They were especially exasperated with sheepdogs which sat quietly with the hill shepherds during the service but dashed about the church when their masters stood for the final blessing, because they thought it was time to go!

Continue on to the Jubilee drinking fountain in the wall on the left.

Each year on Whit Sunday, Northumberland National Park organises an afternoon of traditional folk music, song and dance, on the little green opposite.

At the junction, turn left. Walk on up the road.

It is remarkable that such a tiny village has two such imposing churches. The one on the right is St. Peter's Church of England. There has

12

been a building on the site since the 14th century but it has been restored several times in its history. The last rebuilding was after faulty heating equipment caused a devastating fire on Boxing Day 1890.

The churchyard has some of the finest 18th century gravestone carvings in Northumberland including one of a young girl holding hands with a skeleton and another depicting the Dance of Death.

Follow the road round under the old railway arch.

The arch carried the Border Counties Railway up the valley from Falstone Station, to Kielder and beyond into Scotland, where it joined the Carlisle to Edinburgh Railway, the Waverley Line, at Riccarton Junction. The old station, a short distance down the line, is now a Forestry Commission office, but when the railway was running it was a hive of activity as passengers, goods and even sheep were seen onto and off the trains. Even when there wasn't a train, the station was busy because the station master also ran the coal agency and distributed bulk goods to the farming community.

Turn left up the bank, then immediately right through a field gate. Follow the direction of the waymarkers uphill to the ladder stile over the wall ahead. Cross the stile and keeping the wall immediately on your right follow the waymarked path through the wood.

Although this plantation is mainly Norway spruce it does contain a number of very old specimen conifers, particularly Scots pine, a large tree with very rough bark and also some Norway spruce which has smooth, reddish-coloured bark. These trees probably date back to the 19th century when the main landowners

in the valley, the Duke of Northumberland, Sir John Swinburne and Sir Matthew White Ridley (who owned most of the land round here), began planting timber, notably spruce and pine to supply flooring, pit props and coal staithes to industrial Tyneside.

Many of the younger spruce have been brashed, their lower branches cut off so that the foresters can evaluate the timber. Resin oozing from the wounds leaves distinctive white stains on the bark.

Continue on; cross a small stone bridge over a drainage ditch, go steeply uphill towards the wall and after a short distance the path leads into a birch wood.

This lovely old woodland with its diverse flora provides a marked contrast to the conifer plantation with its sterile floor. The birch has grown naturally from seed blown in by the wind and when it germinated and grew, it was protected by the enclosure wall from grazing animals.

Birch woodland

Birch woods are a good habitat for seed-eating birds and also for fungi. One species of fungi which can be found throughout the year, is the birch polypore, a bracket fungus growing on the trunks of mature trees. Polypore is one of the main causes of death in British trees; most are infected by the time they are around 60 years old.

Birch Polypore

Cross the broken-down wall ahead and follow the waymarkers to join a broad grass track which eventually becomes a forest road. Bear left at the next junction and follow the road round until Kielder Water comes into sight.

This is probably one of the best views of the reservoir. The grass-covered dam wall is in the foreground and the building in the water just beyond, is the valve tower which monitors and regulates the water level. The reservoir is 11km (7 miles) long, 48m (158 feet) deep and holds 44,000 million gallons of water.

Looking half left, due south, on the edge of a clear area in the forest is Smales Farm. Here in 1926 the Forestry Commission planted their very first 18 hectares (45 acres) of land which ultimately became the largest man-made forest in Western Europe. Today Kielder Forest covers 62,000 hectares (153,000 acres).

Carry on. At the waymarker turn left off the road and follow the path downhill to another forest road. Turn right, continue to the next junction, turn left and cross the cattle grid. Pause at the top of the rise overlooking the valley.

On the hillside to the right, behind the big ash tree, is an old garden wall, all that is left of Hawkhope Hill Farm. In the mid-1930s before the Forestry Commission bought the land, the farm building included a large farmhouse, an attached cottage, a stable, two byres and a stone-built hayshed. Occupants of the two-seater netty (toilet) in the garden used to leave the door open so they could gaze out over the valley.

There was never any shortage of visitors to Hawkhope. Shepherds and their families from outbye farms such as Emblehope 5 miles away, left their wellies at Hawkhope when they walked to Falstone for the train or for a dance; or stabled their ponies there if they rode in.

Humps and hollows in the ground to the left of the road mark the site of Hawkhope Hill Pit which was another of Sir Matthew White Ridley's business ventures in the 19th century. The pit was still working in the 1930s, employing about three men, but it wasn't profitable and eventually closed.

Follow the road downhill, under the railway arch and back into the village.

Kielder Water from Hawkhope Hill

13

Kielder Castle – Deadwater Fell – The Kielder Stone – Peel Fell – Deadwater – Bellsburnfoot. 20km (12½ miles); about 7 hours

An exhilarating walk for the more adventurous! The route has been way-marked by the Forestry Commission, but it should only be attempted when the weather is settled and visibility good.

Forest tracks and the level route of the disused Border Counties Railway make an easy beginning and an easy end to this walk. It's the middle section with steep ascents and descents over rough ground and a long trek across wild and boggy moorland that is really demanding. But the view and the experience more than repay all the effort needed to get there!

Park at Kielder Castle car park (GR 632936). Leave the car park at the top left-hand corner (north-west) to join a made path. Turn left and follow the path as it winds between the trees, then alongside a field wall to a forest track. Turn left along the track and after a short distance the view opens out to the left to give a glimpse of Kielder village between the trees.

When it was built shortly after the Second World War, Kielder was a new concept in rural housing. The aim was to provide forestry workers and their families with good accommodation and all the facilities an isolated community was likely to need. So the village was given good access roads, safe play areas for children, a community centre and school, a general store and even a social club in Kielder Castle. However no industrial enterprise can afford to stand still. In the early 1970s the Forestry Commission began to streamline its methods of production and the results have been reflected in the declining workforce and the depopulation of the village.

Carry on through the forest until you reach a clear-felled area on the right.

This block was harvested in 1992 and has since been replanted. Harvesting is done by one machine which fells the tree, measures and cuts the timber to the required length and stacks it nearby. The timber is then taken by another machine called a forwarder, to the roadside ready for collection by timber wagons. The use of machines has drastically reduced the Kielder workforce; harvesters for instance, now do the work of ten men. Moreover by using floodlights on the machinery, timber operations can, if necessary, continue throughout the hours of darkness.

Woodland at Kielder Castle

Follow the track downhill. Turn right at the waymarker and go uphill on a rough track to the stile in the corner of the fence. Cross the stile and make for the line of electricity poles. Then keeping the poles on your right and Lightpipe Sike on your left, cross the tussocky moor to the middle of the low crags ahead. Pause at the rock overhang.

Peden's cave is close by. Alexander Peden was a minister of the Scottish Presbyterian Church. In the 1660s he fled to England to escape persecution and took refuge in remote places in the North Tyne and Rede Valleys. The cave is reputed to be one of his refuges. Here this little man with lank hair and a shrill, squeaking voice held prayer meetings, preached to the local population and baptised William Robson of Emmethaugh. The authorities eventually caught up with Peden on one of his rare visits north of the Border and he was imprisoned for five years on the Bass Rock in the Firth of Forth.

Go left of the cave, make your way up over the rocks, across rough ground again and past another electricity pole to the fence. Turn right and walk up the fenceline to the stile. Cross the stile onto the forest road. Turn right uphill and when you have gained more height stop and look back over the valley.

The stretch of water in the distance is Bakethin Reservoir which feeds the main reservoir, Kielder Water. During the eighteen months it took to build Bakethin dam, the North Tyne had to be diverted through a culvert 73m (240 feet) long. The culvert now runs under the dam and is used to release water periodically from Bakethin to Kielder Water. Bakethin holds 233 million gallons of water. It took only seven days to fill Bakethin to capacity: a graphic indication of the amount of rain which falls in this part of Northumberland!

Continue on to the top of Deadwater Fell. Walk past the triangulation pillar and the RAF radar installations to the end of the road. Find somewhere to sit – a comfy rock or springy clump of heather – and admire the view.

Looking straight ahead from the road end is Peel Fell, at 602m (1975 feet), the highest hill in this range. The border with Scotland runs across the top. To the right and slightly lower is Mid Fell with a cairn on its summit and further right again, the valley of the Kielder Burn and East Kielder Farm with distinctive green fields. To the left of Peel Fell is part of Wauchope Forest in Scotland and further left the valley of the Liddel Water, heading down to Liddesdale, home of the infamous Scottish reivers, the Elliots and Croziers.

From the end of the road go to the corner of the fence. Turn right downhill, cross the stile and follow the path marked by the line of metal/wood fenceposts over Deadwater Moor, past a peaty pool on the left, to the cairn on the top of Mid Fell.

The cairn is believed to be Bronze Age (about 2000 – 700 BC) but only excavation by modern methods will prove or refute this theory.

Bear left at the cairn and continue on the waymarked path towards Peel Fell until you reach a large wooden post about 229m (250 yards) below the summit. The post is on the line of the English/Scottish border and was once part of a fence which has virtually disappeared.

Kielder Water from Elf Kirk

Cottongrass

START

KIELDER CP

West Kielder Moor

Deadwater Moor

Ravenshill Moor

Bells Moor

Myredykes Plantation

1 kilometre

0.5 mile

64

The high moorland you are about to cross is in the Kielderhead Moor Site of Special Scientific Interest (SSSI). It is managed by a small committee headed by Forest Enterprise which owns the land. The area is important for its special plant communities; only the hardiest can survive in such a bleak, exposed place. Purple-flowering heather carpets the peaty soil and cottongrass grows in profusion, its soft, downy flower-heads are a sea of white in early summer. Cloudberry and bilberry can be found here too. More difficult to find is cowberry with its shiny, dark-green leaves and tiny bell-like flowers.

Cowberry

Birds of these open fells include nationally and internationally important colonies of golden plover as well as redshank which breed here from March to July. Their calls are the most haunting and far-carrying of sounds, intended to be heard across wide estuaries as well as open moors. Please keep to the waymarked route especially at this sensitive time of year.

Turn right at the large wooden post and follow the fenceposts over boggy ground and onto a well-defined path leading into Kielder Stone Cleugh. After about 1km you suddenly look down on the 'Mighty Kielder Stone.'

The massive isolated block of Fell Sandstone is about 40m (113 feet) round its circumference and weighs about 1500 tons.

Because the Kielder Stone was such a significant feature in the landscape, it was held in superstitious awe by the local population. In the early 14th century the young Laird of Kielder broke his luck by riding three times round the stone 'widdershins' (anti-clockwise) instead of clockwise and subsequently met a terrible fate at the hands of wicked Lord Soulis of Hermitage Castle.

Later when wars between England and Scotland and the harassing activities of the reivers made it unsafe to travel far, families divided by the Border left messages for each other in crevices in the Kielder Stone – Britain's oldest post box!

The Kielder Stone

The wild Borderlands from Peel Fell

Follow the path back to the large post below the summit of Peel Fell. Turn right and keeping to the fence line, head for the top and the grass-grown summit cairn. From here take the waymarked route across the exposed peat, bearing left to two round posts on the crest of the fell.

Under clear conditions the views are really outstanding. This is one of the few places in Britain where it is possible to see both the east and west coasts. Straight ahead (west), you are looking into Scotland; beyond the forest are the bare fells of Liddesdale and the Tarras Water. To the left (south-west), are the distant waters of the Solway Firth (48km/30 miles) and left again (south) the high peaks of Skiddaw and Blencathra in the Lake District; to the right (north) the broad valleys of the Rivers Teviot and Tweed and further right still (east), the long back of Cheviot and the far-off grey North Sea (64km/40 miles).

From here, the route is all downhill. Descend Peel Fell keeping the line of the ruined wall to your left until you reach the trees. Continue on for about 320m (350 yards) to a waymarked grassy ride on the left. Turn left and after a short distance you meet a forest track. Follow this track downhill, ignoring other tracks to the left and right, to the Deadwater Burn. Pause to scan the heights.

You may be lucky enough to see the wild goats that roam these fells. They aren't wild in the true sense of the word; they are most probably descended from farmyard escapees (or releases!) but they have been around for so long that they are accepted as wild. The goats are small, both sexes have horns and with their shaggy coats, a mixture of black, brown, grey and white, they are well-camouflaged.

Continue to the fork, bear right and carry on downhill to the main road. Turn right, continue until you are opposite the end of the plantation on the far side of the road. Cross the road and follow the waymarked path between the trees up onto the disused railway track over the two-arched bridge.

The Border Counties Railway ran along here until the line was closed in 1958. Because the line cut through many farms provision had to be made for access. The cattle arches, sheep creeps, culverts, crossings and bridges, like this two-arched bridge, are a tribute to the skill of the Irish, English and Scottish navvies who built the railway.

One of the steam engines which puffed up and down this line was The Dipper, named after that distinctive bird of the upland burns. In 1879, The Dipper took 90 people to their deaths in the deep water of the River Tay when the bridge collapsed. The engine was eventually lifted and restored for use on the

Border Counties line but many drivers refused to take it out.

Turn right. Continue along the track for just over 4km (2½ miles). Go past Bellsburnfoot Cottage on the right and carry on down the tree-lined track. Fork left when you meet a forest track and continue round to join the tarmac road. Turn right and walk for 200m (218 yards). Cross the road into Kielder Camp Site and continue on the track. Bear right past the barrier, cross the bridge and turn left. Follow the path uphill past the play area. At the top, bear right and take the forest track back to Kielder Castle car park.

Class D30 "Ellangowan" near Deadwater around 1952

Kielder Castle

14

Byrness – Ogre Hill – The Heart's Toe – Brown Knowe.
11.5km (7 miles); about 4½ – 5 hours

At certain times of the year weather conditions in this area can be quite severe. The highest point, Raven's Knowe is just under 527m (1600 feet) so choose a fine, settled day for this walk.

The outward route follows the Pennine Way. There is a gradual but steep climb to the top of Byrness Hill, then out onto high moorland before descending over boggy ground to the border fence. Thereafter the going is rough in places but with superb views over the border hills to the north. The return leg to Byrness is on forest tracks and rides.

Part of the route is within the Ministry of Defence Otterburn Training Area but the path is open to the public at all times.

Park by the little church of St. Francis on the south side of the A68 (GR 772024).

Go up to the main road, turn left and after about 91m (100 yards) cross the A68 carefully. Go up the tarmac path, pass Byrness cottage and at the Pennine Way sign, turn right through a wicket gate. Follow the path around the edge of the field, go through the wicket gate on the right and into the pinewood.

This fine stand of Scots pine, the only timber-producing conifer native to Britain, should yield a good crop. Scots pine has been growing here for the last 9,000 years, but its once extensive natural cover has been drastically reduced over the centuries by climatic change to warmer and wetter conditions and by man and his grazing animals and it is now confined

to the Scottish highlands. Apart from a few aged remnants along hedgerows, the only pinewoods found in Northumberland today are those grown for their amenity value or grown commercially like this.

Keep on, cross a forest track and continue uphill.

The path now passes through a stand of Norway spruce, the traditional Christmas tree, best identified by its evergreen needle-like leaves set singly on little woody pegs.

Introduced from Norway in the 16th century it is one of the principal commercially-grown conifers best suited to areas of high rainfall. It matures in about 60 years and can reach heights of up to 40m (130 feet), but in this country it is usually harvested when only 40 years old and is used to provide wood pulp rather than timber.

Cross another forest track, go straight on and over a step stile.

Rocks and tree stumps along the path provide a habitat for lichens (pronounced likens) which look like miniature grey-green plants. Lichens are associations of fungae and algae living together and mutually beneficial. The algae produce food for the fungae and in return the fungae provide a protective environment for the algae.

Lichens are important indicators of air quality. This is because they absorb rainwater and if the water contains dissolved chemicals some species of lichens die. Thus the more lichens you see, the purer the air you are breathing.

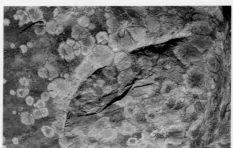

Lichens on rock

Continue on, go over another track and follow the path up between the rocks and boulders. After a short scramble you reach the top of Byrness Hill. Stop and look back.

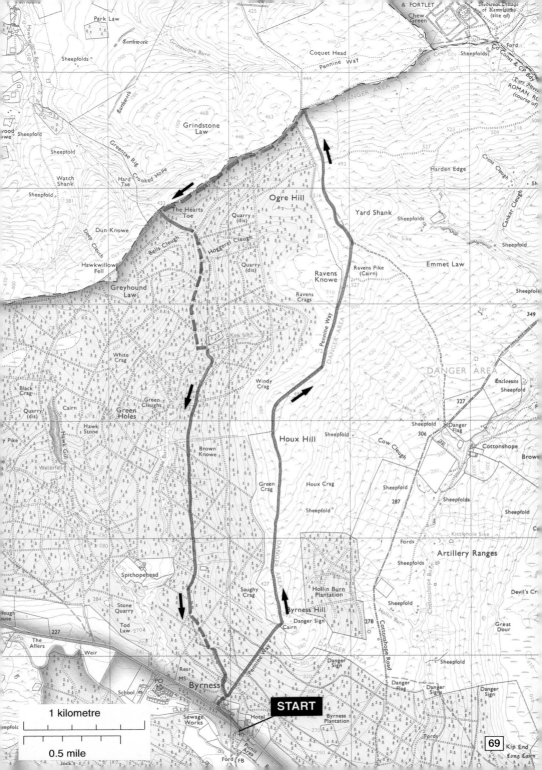

START

69

1 kilometre

0.5 mile

Below, almost surrounded by trees, is Byrness village built in the early 1950s by the Forestry Commission for its workforce and their families. There were 47 houses, shops, a school and village hall. Times change and the men who planted the forest have largely been replaced by machines. Few houses in Byrness are now occupied by foresters while the empty buildings and falling school roll reflect a lack of alternative employment in this remote valley.

To the far right of the village, the stretch of water in the distance is Catcleugh Reservoir which supplies Tyneside. Completed in 1905 by the Newcastle and Gateshead Water Company (now North East Water) Catcleugh is 24m (78 feet) deep, 2km (1½ miles) long and holds 2,345 million gallons of water.

Go through the wicket gate and, keeping the cairn on Byrness Hill on your right follow the Pennine Way along the ridge.

The ridge walk skirts the edge of the Otterburn Training Area – indicated by warning signs – but if you keep to the path you are quite safe.

The views on this next long stretch are quite spectacular. To the left, Catcleugh and the Scottish border; ahead, the Cheviot Hills; to the right, beyond the broad valley of the Cottonshopeburn, the distinctive craggy face of Simonside and right again, on the far horizon, Hadrian's Wall country and the dark line of the Whin Sill.

Continue on over Houx Hill until you reach Raven's Knowe and the corner of the fence on the left.

As you walked along you may have noticed that the vegetation on the far side of the fence is different from that on this side. Heather and bilberry are growing on the ungrazed forest edge whereas here, the fell is virtually all grass. At one time it too would have been heather-covered, but heather can't tolerate over-grazing and the high stocking levels of the 1970s and '80s have led to its disappearance.

Amongst the heather and bilberry are patches of cloudberry. This low, creeping perennial is related to the raspberry and has leaves like the palm of a hand. It is not usually found below 548m (1800 feet). But the high, damp moorland on Raven's Knowe must suit it perfectly.

Continue on to the boardwalk section on the approach to Ogre Hill.

This boardwalk was laid down in 1990 by the National Park. The purpose was to assist vegetation recovery on a very wet area where walkers, attempting to avoid boggy sections of the Pennine Way, had turned the path into a morass up to 14m (15 yards) wide. The work, funded by the Countryside Commission, is part of an ongoing project by National Park field staff and Voluntary Wardens to improve the wetter sections of the Pennine Way.

Cloudberry

Roman military earthworks, Chew Green

Head for the top of Ogre Hill.

In the distance to the north-west you can see a group of three prominent hills, the Eildons, in southern Scotland. The Roman name for this landmark was Trimontium (the Three Hills), a name they also gave to the fort they built nearby. Further right, in the middle distance, is the flat-topped hill of Hownam Law, the site of an Iron Age fort and later Romano-British settlement. Much closer, on the facing slope are the clearly-defined outlines of a complex of Roman military earthworks at Chew Green.

In the 16th century when the Borders were divided into three opposing administrative areas – the East, West and Middle Marches –

for peace-keeping, Chew Green was where the Wardens of the English and Scottish Middle March met to settle grievances against the reivers and to punish those who were caught. Chew Green was chosen because it lay beside the main road into Scotland, Dere Street, the old Roman road. Looking out over these lonely hills now, it is hard to imagine that 400 years ago this was a busy cross-border route.

Go downhill to the fingerpost and take the route signed Permissive Path. Cross the step stile and walk along the edge of the plantation until you meet the forest road.

When Redesdale Forest on the left was planted in the 1960s as an extension of the massive Kielder enterprise, Forestry Commission policy was to grow trees on every part of their holdings even if it meant using wet land.

The forest edge here was planted with lodgepole pine, the conifer thought best suited to survive and thrive in such difficult conditions. This tree is more commonly associated with America where the Indians used it to make a framework on which to erect their lodges or wigwams.

At the road, walk a little further to the gate on the right.

Catleugh Reservoir from Byrness Hill

This is the place to stop and take in the views over the wild border hills. It is a vast and seemingly empty stretch of country. Apart from the Eildon hills which overlook the town of Melrose there is one other distinctive landmark to the north. This is the Wellington monument, a stone tower 46m (150 feet) high on Penielheugh near Jedburgh, about 20km (13 miles) from here.

The foundation stone was laid in 1815 by William Kerr, 6th Marquess of Lothian to commemorate the successes of his mother's cousin the Duke of Wellington on the battlefields of Europe. Unfortunately the building fell down in 1816 before it was completed. Work restarted in 1817 and the monument was eventually finished in 1824. By then however, the Marquess had died.

Immediately opposite the gate follow the waymarked route downhill to the forest road. Turn right and walk along the road for about 1km until you reach a waymarker on the left.

One unusual plant to look for on the right hand side of the road is the stagshorn clubmoss, growing on the exposed gravelly soil on the edge of the drainage ditch. It is a primitive plant which spreads by creeping and rooting. The fruiting capsules (or cones) appear in August, either singly or in pairs on long stalks, creating the impression of a stag's horn – hence the name stagshorn clubmoss.

Stagshorn clubmoss

It is also worth looking for wet flushes on this side of the road where, in late summer you may see lime-loving plants such as the grass of Parnassus.

Turn left at the waymarker and go down through the trees, across a log footbridge and up to the stone-built bothy ahead.

Spithope Bothy renovated by the Mountain Bothies Association together with the Forestry Commission, is run as an open bothy for walkers passing through the area. Originally the bothy was a keb house at the head of the Spithope valley. It was used by local shepherds out on the hills at lambing time and also as a shelter to set on lambs to 'kebbed' (aborted) sheep, or sheep which for some other reason had lost their lambs.

Return to the waymarked path and continue on through the trees to join a green ride. Turn right and follow the ride until it becomes a forest road. Continue on for 2km (1 1/2 miles) through mature conifers.

This section of the walk through the Spithope valley is quite long but these 2km are only a fraction of the 643km (400 miles) of forest road servicing Kielder`s timber production. Over 1000 tons, the equivalent of 50 wagon loads, are extracted daily, 60% of which goes to the paper and pulp-making industry. The rest goes to local sawmills to be made into fencing and wooden pallets.

The road then passes a more open area on the right.

Whenever a new crop is established after clear-felling, a high fence is erected around the trees to protect them from roe deer. Roe, the smallest of our native deer was once absent from Northumberland, the last having been shot at Kielder at the beginning of the century. However, the planting of new forests from the 1920s has proved beneficial to roe deer, with animals moving back from across the border. Their numbers have increased and there are so many today that their browsing habits can damage or deform young trees. To protect these restocked sites, foresters have to erect fences and if necessary cull the deer by shooting.

Keep straight on until you reach the crossing with the Pennine Way. Turn right up the steps then back to the parking place.

Redesdale Ramble

15

High Rochester – Stewartshiels Forest – Sills Burn Valley. 5km (3½ miles); about 2-2½ hours

High Rochester (pronounced Roe-chester) lies near the busy A68. This walk offers the opportunity to explore a part of Redesdale off the beaten track.

Most of the route is over rough hill pasture but the middle section is on forest tracks on Ministry of Defence land where you may meet soldiers on training exercises, or military vehicles. You may also hear gunfire in the distance. The walk however is well clear of target areas so you will be in no danger.

There are no strenuous climbs; the uphill stretches are gradual and the rewards are superb views. The final leg along the banks of the Sills burn is always a pleasure, whatever the weather and it can be quite magical on a crisp winter's day with snow on the ground.

Park on the grass alongside the road which runs through High Rochester (GR 832986).

High Rochester has a long and interesting history. A ferocious raid by Scottish Reivers, the Elliots of Liddesdale in 1583 left the village waste for five years but its main claim to fame are the Roman remains. You are parked within the fort which the Romans called Bremenium (the Place of the Roaring Stream). It was built about AD 80 and for 200 years was the most northerly occupied fort in the Roman Empire. When the Romans eventually withdrew, the local population moved in; some of the barrack blocks were just right for cottages! By the mid 19th century the fort walls, gateways and internal buildings had been dismantled to provide stone for other cottages and field walls round about. All that survives are the outer defences, the grass-covered ramparts, the west gate and part of a turret in the south wall. The central area of the fort is now the village green for Rochester Parish. You are welcome to look around but please remember to close field gates.

The West Gate, High Rochester

Follow the road as it crosses the green towards the row of cottages and then bears right through the field gate. Continue past the sign to Dykehead Farm on the right.

When you have gained a little height pause and look back at High Rochester. From here you get a good view of the fort and its outer defences. Dykehead Farm is in the trees to the left. It is typical of the many small, family-run hill farms in this part of Northumberland. The 988 hectares (400 acres) of rough and improved pasture support a flock of 420 breeding ewes and 50 suckler cows. Grass from the improved fields provides fodder for the stock during winter. The farm's income is derived from the sale of weaned calves for fattening, mule lambs for breeding and fat lambs for slaughter.

Continue to the MoD flag pole on the right. The warning notice does not apply to this route through the Training Area which the MoD have designated as a permissive path.

Leave the road here and go through the field gate in the fence on the right. Cross the sleeper bridge over the burn on the left and then, keeping the burn on your right walk steadily uphill to the waymarker on the skyline.

The steep-sided little valley on the right is called Coal Cleugh because local people dug there for fuel in times gone by. Hollows in the near bankside mark the site of their diggings;

the coal outcrop can be seen near the bottom of the exposed face of the far bank. At the waymarker, the view looking back includes Redesdale Army Camp in the middle distance and on the horizon Rooken Edge, the ridge which forms the watershed between the North Tyne and Rede Valleys.

Keep on for a short distance to the head of the burn, then bear slightly right across rough ground to the next waymarker on the skyline.

This area is dominated by mosses and sedges, creating a suitable habitat for one of Britain's most secretive birds, the snipe. It stays hidden until almost underfoot, when it suddenly rises, flying in erratic zig-zags until out of range and takes cover again. In spring the snipe can be identified by its elaborate display flight. It rises steeply then dives, twisting and turning, whilst making a 'drumming' sound as air vibrates through its tail feathers.

Following the same line of direction make for the fence ahead and cross the stile.

You are now entering Stewartshiels Forest. Beyond the forest the view embraces a vast

Snipe

and seemingly empty landscape. To the left, in the far distance, are Cheviot and Hedgehope, Northumberland's highest hills. To their right are the hills of Upper Coquetdale and right again, the craggy outline of Simonside. Most of this land, virtually as far as the eye can see, is owned by the MoD and is part of the Otterburn Training Area.

Follow the path downhill through the clear-felled area. Cross the sleeper bridge over the drain and after a few yards you reach the track. Turn left and at the T- junction, left again onto a forest road.

The re-planting of Stewartshiels Forest is one

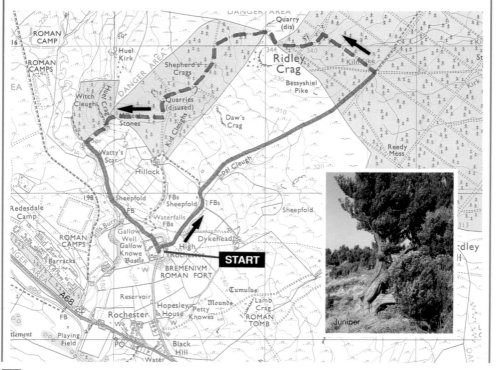
Juniper

of the largest woodland conservation schemes to be carried out in upland Britain. In the 1940s the Forestry Commission planted the whole 2753 hectares (1114 acres) with Sitka and Norway spruce for pit props. When the Commission shed some of its holdings in the 1980s, the MoD bought Stewartshiels but because such dense woodland has little value for military training, conservation or quality of landscape, it was decided that after clear-felling, the area would be replanted with a large percentage of broadleaved trees.

The restructured forest now consists of twelve small woods planted with ash, oak, rowan, hazel and bird cherry, with mainly willow and alder along the water courses. Coniferous species such as Scots pine, Douglas fir, larch and juniper have been planted in the more exposed areas and to give shelter to the less hardy broadleaves. There is provision for ponds and for clearings which can be lightly grazed by sheep and deer.

In time the forest will be of greater use for military training but already it has created new habitats for wildlife and makes a more visually attractive landscape. By agreement with the National Park the MoD has undertaken not to fire live ammunition within the plantation, to preserve the existing public footpath and to grant the permissive path linking the rights of way used in this walk.

Reaching the top of the hill turn left, signed Redesdale Camp. Follow the road out of Stewartshiels and, just before it enters the Shepherd's Crag plantation, stop by the field gate on the right.

The view here looks across bleak countryside, described in reiving days as 'the wastes of Redesdale', towards Thirlmoor at the head of Coquetdale. The long, flat ridge is Houx Hill and to the left on the horizon, Carter Fell the border between England and Scotland.

The poles on either side of the road are for indicating the verges in snowy weather.

Continue down the road until you reach a disused quarry site on the left.

Quarry sites like this are a feature of many conifer forests. Before trees were planted, access roads had to be put in and local

View west from Ridley Crags

sandstone outcrops provided a ready source of road-making material. Here, natural drainage across the quarry floor has created a fresh-water pond which attracts frogs, newts and dragonflies in the breeding season.

Carry on past the entrance to a quarry site on the right and after a few yards leave the road at the waymarker and turn right into the wood. Follow the waymarked path through the trees.

Keep your eyes open for red squirrels along the way. Small heaps of stripped pine cones on the woodland floor indicate their presence. The leaf litter provides a habitat for many species of fungi. Most can only be seen in autumn but several members of the tiny Marasmia family grow here throughout the year.

At the far side of the wood, cross the stile over the perimeter fence and bear right in the direction indicated by the waymarker. Continue over rough ground until you reach the derelict wall and fence. Turn left and, keeping the fence on your right make your way downhill towards the road. Cross the sleeper bridge over the ditch, then the road and go straight ahead to the next way-marker above the bank of the Sills Burn. Turn left and follow the burn down the valley.

This is a pleasant walk along the waterside and if you are here in summer take your time just to look, listen and smell! The valley is rich in wild-life; there are brown trout in the peaty waters of the Sills Burn and the treetops attract small flocks of siskin, searching for seeds among the alder cones and birch catkins. Flowers of every hue from the delicate white and green wood sorrel to the bold pink of ragged robin, pepper the slopes and grass-hoppers noisily advertise their presence by their chirping song.

When you reach the fence, cross the stile by the gate. Bear slightly left onto an old grass-covered track which runs parallel to the Sills Burn and passes a solitary hawthorn tree. Cross the wooden bridge over the small feeder burn and go straight uphill on the clearly-defined track to the corner of the field wall on the skyline. High Rochester is immediately ahead. Keeping the burn on your left, make for the left-hand corner of the fort wall and from there continue to the road. Turn right through the gate and back to your car.

⟨ The Sills Burn (Inset: Squirrel's feeding station)

Elsdon – Landshot – East Nook – Todholes. 8km (5 miles); about 2½ hours

One steep ascent otherwise an easy walk along single track roads and over fields to return to explore the historic village of Elsdon. It is said that the grooves on the pillars inside the door of St. Cuthbert's Church were made by local reivers 'the wild men of Redesdale', who sharpened their swords and daggers on the stonework before setting out to do 'a little shifting (thieving) for their living'.

Park at the north end of the village, by the bridge over the Elsdon Burn (GR 938934). Take the route signed Landshot/Wiskershiel /Eastnook/Hudspeth. Go through the metal gate and up the tarmac road.

The high, grassy mound to the far left is known locally as The Mote Hills. The name is derived from the motte and bailey castle built here in the 12th century. This huge earthworks overlooking the village of Elsdon is one of the finest examples of an early Norman fortification in the whole of England.

Continue on and at the junction, follow the sign to Landshot.

The earliest reference to Landshot is in a 1528 document sent by Henry, Earl of Northumberland, Warden General of the Marches, to Henry VIII's chief minister Cardinal Thomas Wolsey. It lists the names of the inhabitants of Redesdale, among them Hobb (Robert) Hedley of Lanslawgate (Landshot) and his two sons John and William. There are still Hedleys in the district today. Landshot is also mentioned in James I's Border Survey 1604, as one of the wintersteeds in Elsdon Parish. Wintersteeds were cultivated fields near the farm steading, used for winter grazing.

Pass the farmhouse and the converted shepherd's cottage on the left. At the corner of the fence turn left and cross the ladder stile over the wall.

From here, the pattern of rigg and furrow cultivation dating to medieval times is clearly visible on the hillside opposite. The fields, called landshots, were not enclosed by hedges, walls or fences but each was separated from the next by a strip of unploughed land known as a headland. The fact that cultivation was taking place so far up the hill, suggests that the climate in medieval times must have been more favourable than it is now.

Walk downhill and over the footbridge. Cross this, turn left and walk uphill, keeping the wall on your right. Pause at the wicket gate near the top of the hill and look back at the view.

This is one of many places in the National Park offering a tremendous sense of space. Far away to the left are the communication towers on Ottercops. To the right, the distinctive flat-topped mound is the spoil heap from Blaxter quarry; to the right again is the high ridge dividing the Rede and the North Tyne valleys. On the far horizon ahead, the long back of Carter Fell on the border between England and Scotland. Moving round, the remote and empty moorland as far as the eye can see is but a small part of the Ministry of Defence Otterburn Training Area.

Go past the wicket gate to the corner of the wall. Turn right and keeping the wall on your right continue on until you reach another ladder stile on your right.

Gorse

Here the moorland is fringed with gorse bushes. Gorse comes from the Anglo-Saxon word 'gorst' meaning wasteland. In Northumberland gorse is more commonly known by its Scandinavian name whin. In early spring, the vivid yellow flowers can often transform the landscape. Myriads of insects are attracted by the sweet scent (like coconut!) and birds such as yellowhammer and linnet raise their young in the safety of the dense, prickly stems.

Cross the stile and follow the direction of the waymarker arrow to the stone step stile in the wall ahead. Go over the stile and continue straight on, keeping the edge of the conifer plantation on your left.

The way passes through a remnant of heather moorland. Apart from its scenic beauty, this is an important habitat for several species of plants, insects and ground-nesting birds. Hill sheep find the young shoots of heather very nutritious, especially in winter when grass is scarce.

Heather moors were characteristic of the upland landscape not so long ago, but since the Second World War afforestation, improvement for grazing and especially over-stocking have led to their decline. Uncontrolled burning has also contributed to the loss of heather moorland.

To redress the balance, farmers are now advised to follow a more careful programme of heather burning, which regulates the areas to be burnt and the time of year when burning can take place. This creates a continuous supply of new vegetation both for sheep and grouse (managed for sporting purposes). It also reduces damage to the soil and prevents destruction of wildlife habitats. But burning alone will not safeguard heather moorland, the only sure way is to reduce stocking levels.

Go over the stone step stile near the corner of the wall and, with the wall on your left, make towards East Nook, the farm in the trees ahead. Go past a gate in the wall on your left to another stone step stile and follow the fence on your right to a step stile at the roadside. Cross the stile and turn right onto the road.

The trees to the left of the road are ash, which comes from the Anglo-Saxon 'aesc' meaning spear. Because of its toughness ash was used to make shafts for spears and lances.

Female red grouse

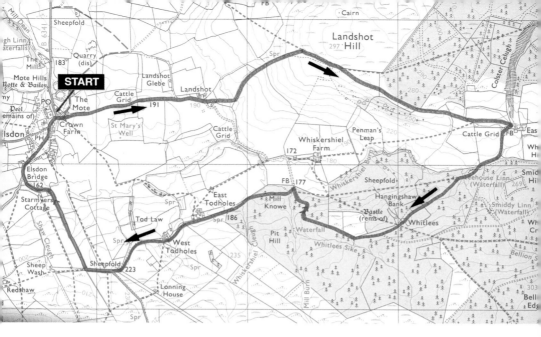

Ash was also reputed to have healing properties. It was claimed to cure anything from whooping cough and hernia to bed-wetting and warts. The treatment for ulcerated ears for instance, was to boil ash keys in the patient's urine, soak some black wool in the liquid then place the wool in the sore ear and say "By God's help, it will cure it!" Unfortunately no 13th century patient left a record to say whether this remedy was a success!

Continue along the tarmac road, over a cattle grid, through a metal gate and uphill towards Whitlees.

Several species of conifer have been planted in blocks along either side of the road, Sitka spruce, Norway spruce, Scots pine and larch. Such plantations may look dull but they are vibrant and alive with all manner of creatures. The forest aspect and its wildlife are continually changing as the trees grow.

Walk past the front of Whitlees and stop at the end of the garden wall. Look over the paddock to the building on the far side.

Ash tree in autumn

This bastle, reduced in height is now used as a store. The large double door in the wall facing and the attached byres to the left are a relatively recent addition. The original features include the massive masonry and the small,

square window with a chamfered surround
and a grille of iron bars.

**Continue along the road as it gradually
descends, through the trees. At the bottom
of the hill turn left at the fingerpost signed
Bridleway and follow the path through the
trees to the Mill Burn.**

Reputed to be the prettiest burn in Northumberland, the Mill Burn is leased by the Tillhill
Forestry Group to Northumberland Wildlife
Trust to manage as a nature reserve. The burn
flows across an outcrop of the Four Laws
Limestone, which supports an interesting flora
including the insectivorous butterwort.

Butterwort

**Cross the burn and walk up through the
forest ride ahead. At the end of the ride, go
through the gate and continue on past East
Todholes.**

Todholes, like all the other farmsteads in this
valley, is also mentioned in 16th century
documents. Tod, meaning fox, is probably an
Anglo-Saxon word and its frequent use in
place names is evidence that foxes were as
widespread then as they are now.

**At the top of the hill the farm road levels
out. Pause and look over to Elsdon village
on the right.**

This is probably the best view of the Mote Hills.
The circular mound where the wooden keep
stood and the rectangular bailey to the right
are prominent landmarks. To the left of the
Mote Hills is the village itself, the houses
grouped around the green and the church and
the stout-walled vicar`s pele tower, the ancient
'turris de Ellysden'.

**At the end of the farm road turn right onto
the main road. Walk down the road back to
the village.**

Elsdon is one of the most interesting villages in the National Park and is well worth exploring. It has a rare combination of superb historic and architectural features including the green with its pinfold, an overnight enclosure for stock, the church with its graveyard memorials and perhaps the best range of small Georgian buildings in any village in Northumberland.

The Vicar's Pele, Elsdon

Glossary

Bastle defensible farmhouse. **Burn** small river or stream. **Cairn** heap of stones marking a summit or prehistoric grave. **Fell** hill. **Haugh** flat land by a river or burn. **Inbye** improved land near the farm buildings. **Knowe** small hill or moorland slope. **Lough** lake. **Midden** refuse heap. **Mire** (moss) peat bog. **Outbye** unimproved land furthest away from the farm buildings. **Set** paving block. **Shiel (Shield, Shieling)** summer grazing ground or simple huts used there. **Sike (Syke)** ditch or small burn.

Further Reading

The Steel Bonnets George Macdonald Fraser *Barrie and Jenkins Ltd 1971*

Upper North Tynedale Beryl Charlton *Northumbrian Water 1987*

Northumberland National Park Tony Hopkins *Webb and Bower 1987*

Hadrian's Wall D. J. Breeze and B. Dobson *Penguin 1976*

Reiving Families

The reivers were robbers and thieves. In the 15th and 16th centuries economic and social conditions on the Borders were such that there were too many mouths to feed and not enough food or gainful employment. To survive, people stole from each other and, to make their raids successful, banded together in kinships (families) or groups of kinships. These raids led to inter-family hatred which resulted in blood feuds lasting several generations.

The main kinships in the area covered by this book were:

Redesdale Anderson, Brown, Coxon, Dagg, Dunn, Fletcher, Forster, Hall, Hedley, Reed, Spoor.

North Tynedale (including Kielder) Armstrong, Charlton, Corbett, Dodd, Elliot, Hunter, Milburn, Robson.

Hadrian's Wall Ridley, Thirlwell.

Notes